AFRICA

Tafraout, an oasis in Morocco

The World in Maps

AFRICA

Martyn Bramwell

Lerner Publications Company • Minneapolis

**First American edition published in 2000
by Lerner Publications Company**

© 2000 by Graham Beehag Books

Lerner Publications Company
A division of Lerner Publishing Group
241 First Avenue North
Minneapolis, MN 55401 U.S.A.

Website address: www.lernerbooks.com

Library of Congress Cataloging-in-Publication Data

Bramwell, Martyn.
    Africa / by Martyn Bramwell
        p. cm. — (The world in maps)
    Includes index.
    Summary: Text and maps present the location, topography, climate, population, industries, languages, and currencies of Africa.
    ISBN 0-8225-2914-9 (lib. bdg.)
    1. Africa—Juvenile literature. [1. Africa.] I. Title. II. Series.
DT22. B73 2000
960—dc21   00-008050

Printed in Singapore by Tat Wei Printing Packaging Pte Ltd
Bound in the United States of America
1 2 3 4 5 6 – OS – 05 04 03 02 01 00

Picture credits
Pages 17, 23, 32 Robert Estall

CONTENTS

20° 10° 0° 10° 20° 30° 40° 50° 60°

Madeira I.

Canary Is.

MOROCCO

TUNISIA

MEDITERRANEAN SEA

Persian Gulf

ALGERIA

LIBYA

EGYPT

Tropic of Cancer

WESTERN SAHARA

MAURITANIA

MALI

NIGER

CHAD

SUDAN

RED SEA

ERITREA

EGAL

BURKINA FASO

GUINEA

SIERRA LEONE

LIBERIA

CÔTE D'IVOIRE

GHANA

TOGO

BENIN

NIGERIA

CAMEROON

CENTRAL AFRICAN REPUBLIC

ETHIOPIA

DJIBOUTI

Gulf of Aden

SOMALIA

Gulf of Guinea

Bioko

EQUATORIAL GUINEA

São Tomé and Príncipe

GABON

Cabinda

REPUBLIC OF THE CONGO

UGANDA

KENYA

DEMOCRATIC REPUBLIC OF THE CONGO

RWANDA

BURUNDI

TANZANIA

Zanzibar

INDIAN OCEAN

ATLANTIC OCEAN

SEYCHELLES

Comoros

Mayotte

ANGOLA

ZAMBIA

MOZAMBIQUE

MADAGASCAR

Mozambique Channel

ZIMBABWE

NAMIBIA

BOTSWANA

Tropic of Capricorn

SWAZILAND

SOUTH AFRICA

LESOTHO

500   1000   1500   2000 Miles

1000   2000   3000 Km

6

20° 10° 0° 10° 20° 30° 40° 50°

AFRICA

Above: Most North Africans are Muslims, who worship in mosques like the magnificent Koutubia Mosque in Marrakech, Morocco. A muezzin (crier) calls the faithful to prayer from the ornate minaret (tower).

Below: Wildebeest thunder across the open grasslands of South Africa's Rooipoort Game Reserve.

Africa is the second-largest continent by land area (11.7 million square miles) and the third largest by population (771 million people). The continent is a patchwork of more than 50 countries, each with many different people, languages, and customs. Africa's population is spread unevenly across the land. The desert countries of Libya and Mauritania have only about 7 people per square mile, while Nigeria, the most crowded country, supports 319 people per square mile.

The continent stretches 5,000 miles north to south—from the warm shores of the Mediterranean Sea to the cold stormy waters off the Cape of Good Hope—and 4,700 miles west to east, from the Atlantic coast of Senegal to Somalia, which juts into the Indian Ocean. Three major mountain ranges skirt the continent. The Atlas Mountains rise to 13,671 feet in the northwest. Africa's highest peak, Mount Kilimanjaro, at 19,341 feet, towers over East Africa's high plateau. The Drakensberg Mountains rise 11,425 feet above sea level in eastern South Africa and Lesotho.

The Great Rift Valley, Africa's most spectacular landscape feature, is a huge crack in the earth's crust that cuts through the continent for 4,300 miles from the Red Sea to Malawi. Africa embraces some of the world's most noted water features. Lake Victoria, covering 26,828 square miles, is in area the world's second-largest freshwater lake after Lake Superior. The Nile, snaking along for 4,160 miles, is the world's longest river. And Victoria Falls on the Zambia–Zimbabwe border rushes around three islands before plunging 350 feet.

Africa has vast forest resources, as well as huge reserves of copper, diamonds, gold, and petroleum. But most African countries lack the money and skilled workers needed to build and run factories. South Africa, Egypt, Morocco, Algeria, and Nigeria are the only African countries with well-developed industries. Most African families depend on **subsistence agriculture,** growing just enough to feed themselves. Farmers in more fertile areas often grow **cash crops** for export. Large-scale plantations, owned mostly by multinational companies, produce cacao beans, coffee beans, cashews, cloves, bananas, vanilla, tea, cotton, and sugar.

Morocco and Algeria

Morocco

Status:	Constitutional Monarchy
Area:	172,413 square miles
Population:	28.2 million
Capital:	Rabat
Languages:	Arabic, Berber, French, Spanish
Currency:	Dirham (100 centimes)

Algeria

Status:	Republic
Area:	919,591 square miles
Population:	30.8 million
Capital:	Algiers
Languages:	Arabic, Berber, French
Currency:	Algerian dinar (100 centimes)

Morocco is bordered by the Atlantic Ocean to the west and the Mediterranean Sea to the north. The two coastlines are separated by a rocky headland that juts toward Spain to form the narrow Strait of Gibraltar. Well-watered fertile plains stretch along the coasts, where farmers produce wheat, barley, corn, sugar beets, beans, fruits, and vegetables. Major landowners control about one-third of the farmland and account for 85 percent of all the crops produced. Most Moroccan farmers get by on a few acres, raising crops and tending sheep, goats, and dairy cattle. Morocco is one of Africa's leading fishing nations. Sardines, mackerel, and tuna are caught and then canned for export or converted into animal feed or fertilizer.

Morocco has about two-thirds of the world's reserves of phosphate rock, which is mined and exported for making fertilizer and other chemical products. The country also has reserves of iron ore, copper, lead, and zinc, but most of the country's energy is based on imported oil.

Casablanca, Morocco's main manufacturing center, produces cement, chemicals, fertilizers, paper, plastics, leather goods, and processed foods.

Nearly half of Algeria's people live in cities and towns on the narrow coastal plain bordering the Mediterranean Sea. Here the climate is warm, with mild winters and up to 30 inches of rain each year. Farmers in this region grow cereal grains, vines, olives, fruits, and vegetables and raise sheep, goats, and cattle. About 30 percent of Algerians work in factories in Algiers, Annaba, Constantine, Skikda, and other cities on or near the coast. These manufacturing centers produce iron and steel, construction materials, textiles, phosphate fertilizers, and refined petroleum products. The country is rich in oil and natural gas, but political unrest has prevented the government from making full use of these resources. As a result, many thousands of Algerians go abroad, many of them to France, to find work.

The Atlas Mountains rise steeply behind the coastal plain, separating the mild northern region from the hot dry Sahara Desert, which covers 80 percent of the country. The northern Sahara is mainly sand. To the south and east, it is bare rock and boulders. Less than 3 percent of Algerians live in the desert. A few are oil field workers, and some live in scattered oases where dates and cereal grains can be grown. The remainder are nomadic Tuareg people who speak the Berber language and travel between the region's sparse grazing areas with their camels, sheep, and goats.

Right: A natural rock arch in the rugged Tassili Mountains of southern Algeria. Striking landscape features like this are the result of thousands of years of erosion by windblown sand and the flash floods that follow brief but heavy desert rains.

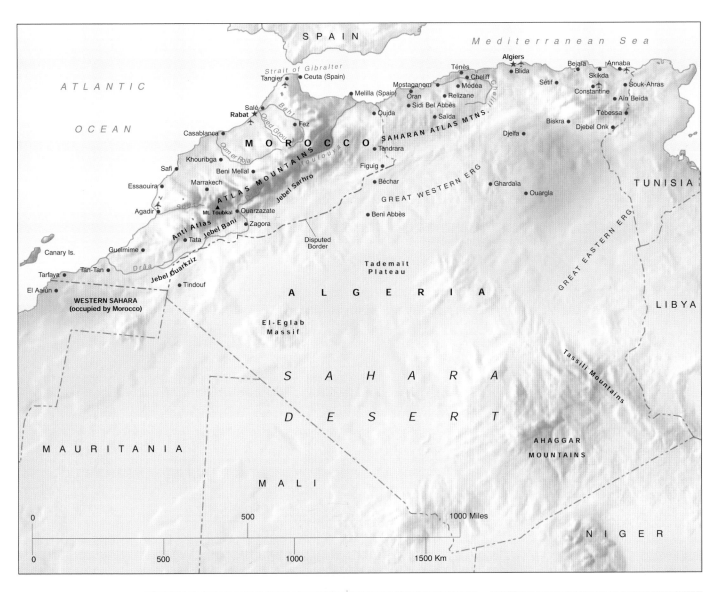

Far right: These Moroccan water sellers are a familiar sight in the hot, dry cities. The water is carried in a goatskin bag slung from the shoulder and is served to customers in highly polished cups made of beaten copper.

Right: Farmers' wives wash freshly picked cotton on the banks of the Oued Grou River at Rabat, Morocco.

Tunisia and Libya

Tunisia

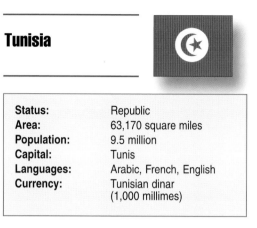

Status:	Republic
Area:	63,170 square miles
Population:	9.5 million
Capital:	Tunis
Languages:	Arabic, French, English
Currency:	Tunisian dinar (1,000 millimes)

Tunisia's northern landscape consists of low mountains with patches of cork oak and evergreen woodland. The Atlas Mountains lie near the Mediterranean coast of this North African nation, and the Tabassah Mountains, part of the same Atlas range, lie farther south. Farmers grow wheat and other grains in the Majardah River Valley and in additional fertile lowlands between the two ranges. A vast, dry, grassy plain lies south of the mountains and is dotted with salt lakes and **pans.** Beyond the plain lies the Sahara Desert.

Tunisia's most productive region is the narrow plain along its eastern coast, where fertile soil and winter rains yield excellent crops of grains, citrus fruits, grapes, melons, and olives. Olive groves cover nearly one-third of the country's farmland, making Tunisia the world's fifth-largest producer of olives and olive oil.

Phosphates and oil are Tunisia's major mineral resources. Both are exported in large quantities. The country's manufacturing centers supply textiles, clothing, paper, steel, construction materials, and processed foods to both local and export markets. Tourism is fast becoming one of Tunisia's most important industries. Although Tunisia suffers frequent droughts and dwindling oil reserves, the government devotes nearly half the national budget to education, health care, and other social services.

Right: Tunisian elders deep in discussion. The decorative tiled wall mosaics, rush matting, and colorful rugs are typical of the culture.

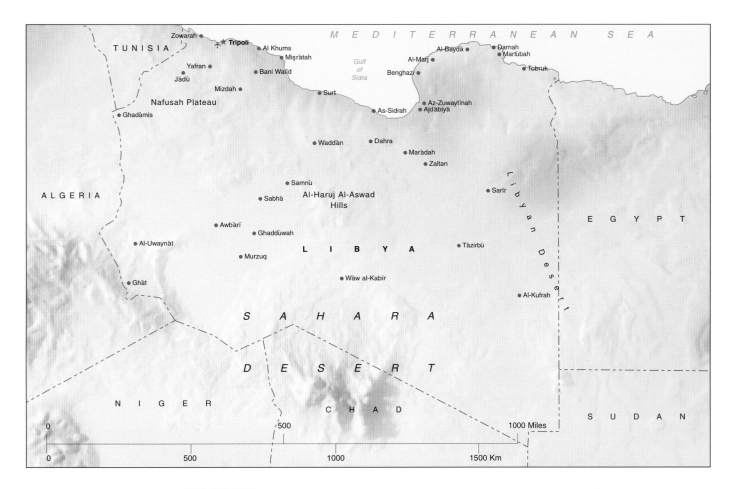

Libya

Status:	Republic
Area:	679,359 square miles
Population:	5.0 million
Capital:	Tripoli
Languages:	Arabic, Berber
Currency:	Libyan dinar (1,000 dirhams)

The Sahara Desert blankets nearly 95 percent of Libya. Vast sand dunes cover much of the country's northern half, gradually giving way to stone-covered desert that rises to a rugged mountain range in the south. Libya's climate is hot and dry, receiving less than two inches of annual rainfall. Of the few Libyans who inhabit this desert area, most live in scattered **oases** and grow dates, grains, and vegetables.

Some work in the desert oil fields. The rest are nomadic herders constantly on the move in search of grazing land for their camels, sheep, and goats.

Most of Libya's people live in towns and villages on the Mediterranean coastal plain, where they enjoy fertile soil, mild temperatures, and up to 16 inches of rain each year. Farmers in this region grow wheat, barley, potatoes, dates, and citrus fruits and raise cattle, sheep, and poultry. Most Libyan farms are small family businesses, so the country imports much of the food it needs to feed its rapidly growing population.

Oil, Libya's principal mineral resource and its most significant export, accounts for about one-quarter of the country's total economic production. Libyans also mine iron ore, lime, gypsum, sulfur, and some natural gas. Oil refineries and factories in the northern cities process foods and produce petroleum and petrochemicals, cement, and some iron and steel.

Above: Sheer rocky cliffs and boulder-strewn plateaus dominate the landscape of southern Libya. To the northeast, in the distance, lie the rolling sand dunes of the Libyan Desert.

Egypt

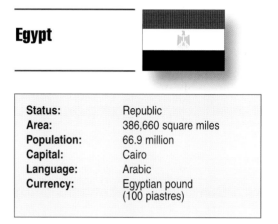

Egypt

Status:	Republic
Area:	386,660 square miles
Population:	66.9 million
Capital:	Cairo
Language:	Arabic
Currency:	Egyptian pound (100 piastres)

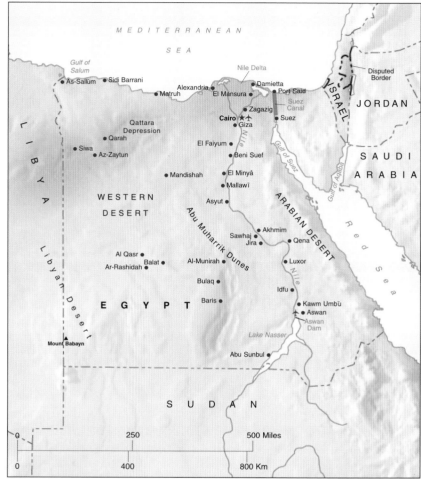

Egypt has the second-largest population in Africa (after Nigeria), and its capital, Cairo, is the continent's most populous city, housing 13 million residents. About 99 percent of Egyptians live on just 4 percent of the land—consisting of the narrow fertile valley of the Nile, the Nile **Delta,** and the banks of the **Suez Canal.**

The Nile River has enabled Egypt to become one of Africa's leading nations. Farmers in the Nile Valley produce nearly all of Egypt's home-grown food including corn, rice, potatoes, wheat, oranges, tomatoes, and sugarcane. These farmers also tend Egypt's most valuable cash crop—high-quality, long-fiber cotton that is exported worldwide. Dams and reservoirs hold back the Nile's waters and provide year-round irrigation.

Sand and rock deserts interspersed with a few salt marshes claim the rest of this North African country. Scattered oases house small communities that grow date palms and vegetables and rear sheep and goats. The deserts are also home to the Bedouin people. Some still follow the traditional nomadic way of life, although many have settled and become farmers.

Egypt is not rich in mineral resources, but petroleum and natural gas, iron ore, manganese, and phosphates are vital exports and provide fuel and raw materials for the country's industries. Cairo and the main port of Alexandria house the country's principal manufacturing centers. Factory goods include petrochemicals, textiles, chemicals, steel, fertilizers, and metal and food products. Cairo is also a major financial center and the launching point for millions of tourists who visit the country's spectacular ancient monuments—the pyramids, the Sphinx, and the Valley of the Kings.

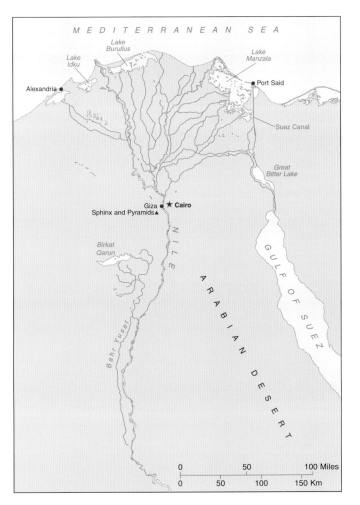

Above: The Nile Valley and its vast river delta are among the world's most fertile regions. This great river irrigates almost six million acres of farmland in Egypt and three million acres in neighboring Sudan.

Above left: The *felucca* is the traditional boat of Nile fishers and traders.

Left: The Sphinx and the great pyramids at Giza are among the most identifiable sights of the ancient world.

Facing page: The Nile River winds through the center of Cairo—the biggest city in Africa and one of the world's fastest-growing urban centers.

Sudan

Sudan

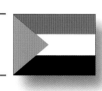

Status:	Republic
Area:	967,494 square miles
Population:	28.9 million
Capital:	Khartoum
Languages:	Arabic, English
Currency:	Sudanese dinar (100 pounds)

Africa's largest country by area, Sudan is a land of contrasts. Northern Sudan is mainly desert, with less than 4 inches of annual rainfall and daytime temperatures consistently above 100°F. The central region is a vast grassy plain that gets slightly more rain. Southern Sudan is hot and humid with 40 inches of rain each year and temperatures averaging 80°F. This southern region is covered in dense forests and swamps that merge with the tropical rain forests of the Democratic Republic of the Congo and the Central African Republic.

Like Egypt to its north, Sudan depends on the Nile River. About 80 percent of its people live in rural areas, most of them farming the valleys of the Nile and its main tributaries—the White Nile and the Blue Nile. But the valleys are not productive enough to feed everyone. Infertile soil leaves many farmers struggling to grow enough food to feed their families. The remaining 20 percent of the population live in Sudan's major cities—the capital city of Khartoum, Omdurman (the biggest city), Wad Medani, Port Sudan, and Juba. Small factories and service industries provide jobs for a majority of the city dwellers.

Agriculture accounts for 40 percent of Sudan's economy. Cotton and **gum arabic** are the principal exports. Sudanese farmers plant millet, sorghum, sugarcane, and vegetables and produce meat and dairy products for local consumption. Miners extract chromium, gold, gypsum, and oil. Urban factory workers make cement, fertilizers, textiles, and leather products for local and international markets.

Above: A trader sells his goods in a traditional market in Khartoum, Sudan.

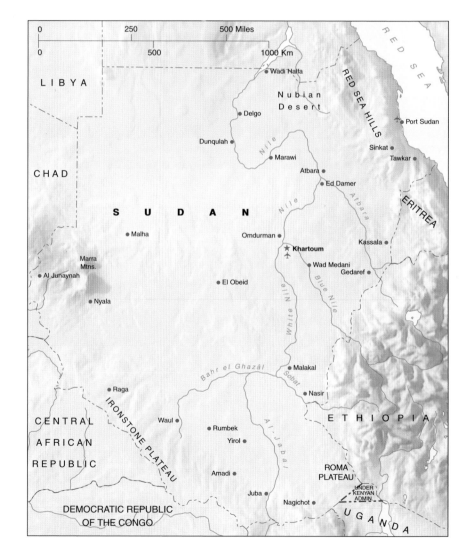

Eritrea and Ethiopia

Eritrea

Status:	Independent State
Area:	45,405 square miles
Population:	4.0 million
Capital:	Asmara
Languages:	Tigrinya, Tigre, Arabic, English
Currency:	Eritrean birr (100 cents)

This former province of Ethiopia has been fought over for centuries. After periods of rule by Italy, Britain, and Ethiopia, Eritrea fell into a bitter civil war in the 1980s and early 1990s. Eritrea formally declared itself, as well as the Dahlak **Archipelago** in the Red Sea, free of Ethiopia in 1993. But the constant conflicts and a succession of severe droughts have devastated this new East African country. Three-quarters of the people depend on foreign food aid, and the country's illiteracy rate is high.

The government in the capital of Asmara is attempting to rebuild Eritrea's economy by supporting traditional textile and leather industries and by developing fishing and tourism. Highland farmers grow sorghum, cotton, **teff**, coffee beans, tobacco, and citrus fruits. The land is not very productive, however, and rainfall is erratic. Eritrea imports food and other goods from neighboring countries. Salt mines in the arid Danakil Depression in the hot, dry eastern region produce the country's most valuable export.

Ethiopia

Status:	Federal Republic
Area:	426,371 square miles
Population:	59.7 million
Capital:	Addis Ababa
Languages:	Amharic, Arabic
Currency:	Ethiopian birr (100 cents)

Rugged mountains and high fertile plateaus veil western Ethiopia, where the highland climate is usually a mild 60°F. Droughts occur and the people are poor, but enough rain falls during most summers for farmers to produce sufficient wheat, corn, sorghum, and teff to feed their families. Most farmers also raise cattle, sheep, goats, and chickens. The richest farmland is in the southwest, where farmers grow commercial crops of oilseed, sugarcane, and coffee beans—the country's biggest export. The Great Rift Valley, which runs north to south through the country, splits the highland region in two. Eastern Ethiopia consists of hot, dry, lowland plains where rainfall seldom exceeds 15 inches, and the temperature averages 80°F. The thermometer can rise to a fierce 120°F in the deserts of the northeast, a largely uninhabited area. Most Ethiopians live in the highlands—85 percent of them in rural villages and scattered farms and the other 15 percent in towns. Addis Ababa, the capital, is home to 2.3 million people.

Ethiopia hosts many different cultures and people, who speak more than 80 languages and 200 dialects. About 40 percent of the people are Ethiopian Orthodox Christians, 40 percent are Muslims, and most of the remainder follow traditional African religions.

Industry is underdeveloped. Ethiopia has few mineral resources, so manufacturing—based mainly in the capital—consists largely of textiles, leather goods, cement, and processed foods. Eritrea's independence left Ethiopia without a coastline, but the two countries reached an agreement allowing Ethiopia to export goods through the Eritrean port of Asseb. Goods are also exported through Djibouti. The long war with Eritrea, a succession of droughts and famines in the 1970s, 1980s, and 1990s, and the effects of deforestation and poor farming methods have left Ethiopia desperately poor and almost completely dependent on international aid.

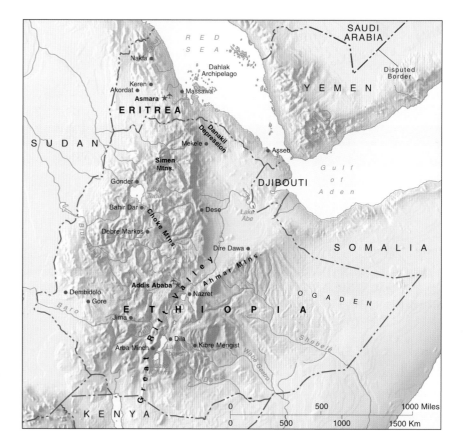

Djibouti and Somalia

Djibouti

Status:	Republic
Area:	8,958 square miles
Population:	600,000
Capital:	Djibouti
Languages:	Arabic, Afar, Somali, French
Currency:	Franc (100 centimes)

Somalia

Status:	Republic
Area:	246,201 square miles
Population:	7.1 million
Capital:	Mogadishu
Languages:	Somali, Arabic, English
Currency:	Shilling (100 cents)

Djibouti is very small, extremely poor, and depends almost entirely on the fact that it has one of the best harbors on Africa's eastern coast—at the nation's capital, also called Djibouti, on the Gulf of Aden. The port is the end point for a railroad built in 1917 by the government of Ethiopia to link Addis Ababa, Ethiopia's capital, to the coast. A large proportion of Ethiopia's foreign trade passes through the port, providing Djibouti with its primary source of income.

More than 90 percent of Djibouti is desert. Its barren coastal plain suffers one of the hottest, driest climates on earth, with less than five inches of annual rainfall and average temperatures around 90°F. Hilly terrain rises to nearly 5,000 feet in the country's north and west, meeting Ethiopia's highlands at the border.

Most of Djibouti's people belong to two main ethnic groups—the Afar in the north and the Issa in the south. Both groups are traditional nomadic herders of camels, sheep, goats, and cattle, but more and more of them are giving up the struggle to live in the barren countryside and are moving to the capital city and highland towns. This influx of people has put pressure on urban resources already strained by the thousands of refugees who have fled to Djibouti from conflicts in Ethiopia and Somalia. Djibouti is also home to many Arab traders and a large French community—a reminder of the country's 100 years under French rule before it gained independence in 1977. Djibouti exports salt and dates but depends heavily on foreign aid.

Somalia, like so many other African countries, gained independence in 1960 after nearly 100 years of shared **colonial rule** between Britain and Italy. But independence did not bring peace. For the last 30 years, Somalia has been torn apart by civil war, conflict with Ethiopia, and severe droughts that have killed nearly half a million people.

Somalia is a hot, dry East African country, covered almost entirely in dry **savanna** grassland. A low mountain range lies across northern Somalia, where average temperatures reach 100°F and annual rainfall can be as little as 3 or 4 inches. Central and southern Somalia feel almost wet by comparison. Annual rainfall in these low, flat regions can exceed 12 inches, and temperatures range from 64°F to 100°F.

Most of the country is too dry and infertile for farming. Two-thirds of Somalis are nomadic herders—grazing their sheep, goats, cattle, and camels wherever they can find enough pasture. In the south, the Jubba and Shabeelle Rivers provide water for irrigation and enable farmers to grow corn, sorghum, cotton, bananas, citrus fruits, and sugarcane. Somalia's main exports are animal hides and leather goods, bananas, and livestock—most of which Saudi Arabia purchases. The country has to import much of its food, the bulk of its manufactured goods, and all of its oil and petroleum.

After nearly 25 years of intense fighting and severe starvation, Somalia allowed in U.S. forces, which hoped to keep the warring factions apart and to ensure that desperately needed food and supplies would reach the starving people. The following year, the United Nations took over the operation, but in 1995 the peacekeepers withdrew, unable to stop the fighting.

Above: Somali nomads draw water for their camels from a deep well in the Ogaden Desert on the country's border with Ethiopia.

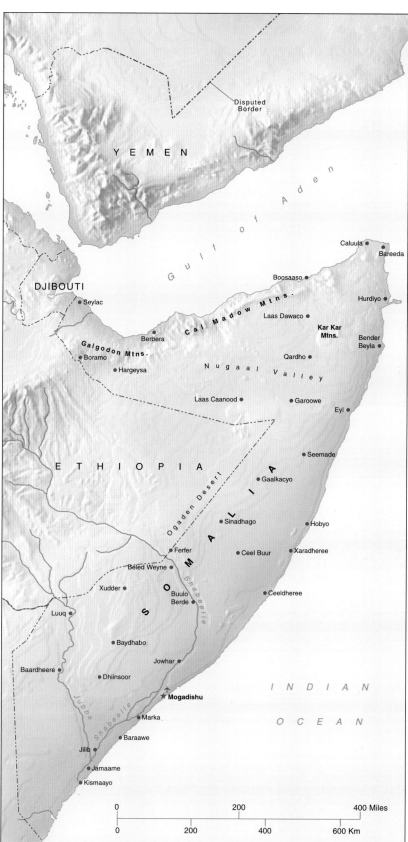

Western Sahara and Mauritania

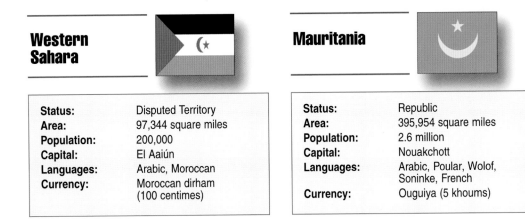

Western Sahara

Status:	Disputed Territory
Area:	97,344 square miles
Population:	200,000
Capital:	El Aaiún
Languages:	Arabic, Moroccan
Currency:	Moroccan dirham (100 centimes)

Mauritania

Status:	Republic
Area:	395,954 square miles
Population:	2.6 million
Capital:	Nouakchott
Languages:	Arabic, Poular, Wolof, Soninke, French
Currency:	Ouguiya (5 khoums)

Western Sahara, formerly Spanish Sahara, lies on Africa's northwestern coast. Most of the country is barren desert dotted with wadis (dry streambeds) that fill briefly after occasional rainstorms but dry out almost immediately. The Saharawi people are mostly Arab and Berber nomads who roam the desert with their herds of camels, sheep, and goats. The inland desert soil is too dry and infertile for agriculture, although small farms on the coast manage to grow grains and vegetables. Fishing crews along the coast catch and dry fish for export to the Spanish-owned Canary Islands, 70 miles off the African coast. Western Sahara's one asset is its huge reserves of phosphate rock, an ingredient in fertilizers. The deposits southeast of the capital of El Aaiún are the largest in the world. The valuable minerals are one of the reasons neighboring states have tried to take control of the country.

Spain established a colony in the area in 1884 but gave up its claim in 1976 under pressure from Morocco and Mauritania. Morocco then ruled the northern part of the territory, and Mauritania governed the south. The Polisario Front—a local independence movement—became the third player in a bitter struggle for control. Mauritania pulled out in 1979, but Morocco still holds power. Since 1992 Morocco has been promising a referendum (a public vote) on whether Western Sahara should become independent, but the process has been deadlocked by disagreements over who is eligible to vote.

Right: Wind-rippled sand dunes cover vast areas of northern Mauritania.

Mauritania bridges two worlds—the Arab world to the north and black African world to the south. Most of the northerners are of Arab and Berber descent who speak Arabic and follow the Islamic faith. A large proportion of black Africans, many of whom are Christians or followers of traditional religions, inhabit southern Mauritania. The country was a French colony from 1903 until it achieved independence in 1960. Military leaders ruled Mauritania until 1991, when the country adopted a new constitution and democratic elections.

The vast sand plains and rocky highlands of the Sahara Desert dominate most of the country. The **Sahel,** a belt of low, arid plains covered in sparse grass and scrub, stretches across Mauritania's southern border. Most of the people living in the Sahel region are nomadic herders. Black Africans, most of them settled farmers, are concentrated in the southwest where the fertile soil of the Senegal River and its tributaries affords premium crops of millet, corn, beans, rice, and dates. Coastal fisheries provide another important source of food and export income. High-grade iron ore mined near Fdérik is Mauritania's most valuable mineral resource. Most of it is exported to Europe. Fish, iron ore, and copper exports do not earn enough to support the economy, and Mauritania depends heavily on foreign aid, much of it from France.

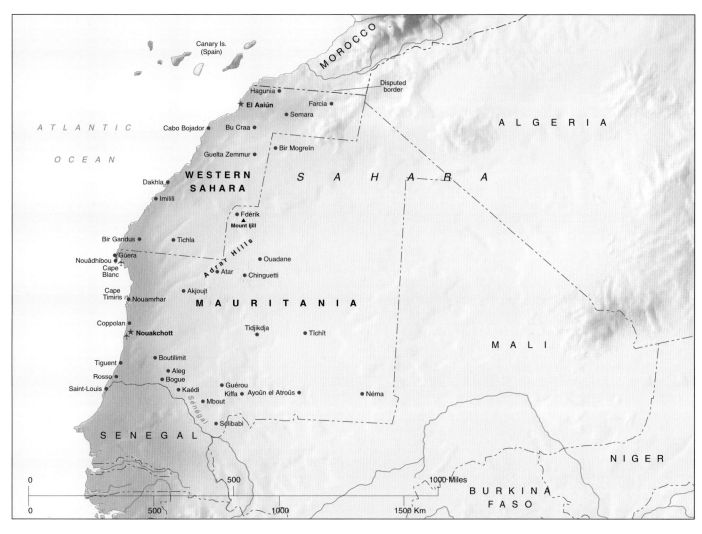

Canary Is.
(Spain)

MOROCCO

Hagunia •

★ **El Aaiún**

ATLANTIC

OCEAN

Farcia •

• Semara

ALGERIA

Cabo Bojador •

Bu Craa •

Guelta Zemmur •

• Bir Mogreïn

**WESTERN
SAHARA**

Dakhla •

S A H A R A

• Imilili

• Fdérik

▲ **Mount Ijill**

Bir Gandus •

• Tichla

Nouâdhibou •
Cape
Blanc

Güera

• Ouadane

Atar •

• Chinguetti

Cape
Timiris •

• Akjoujt

Nouamrhar •

M A U R I T A N I A

Coppolan •

★ **Nouakchott**

• Tidjikdja

• Tîchît

M A L I

Tiguent •

• Boutilimit

Rosso •

• Aleg

• Bogue

Saint-Louis •

• Kaédi

Kiffa •

• Guérou

• Ayoûn el Atroûs

• Néma

• Mbout

N I G E R

• Selibabi

S E N E G A L

Senegal

0

0

500

500

1000

1000 Miles

1500 Km

**B U R K I N A
FASO**

Mali and Burkina Faso

Mali

Status:	Republic
Area:	478,838 square miles
Population:	11 million
Capital:	Bamako
Languages:	French, local languages
Currency:	CFA franc (100 centimes)

Burkina Faso

Status:	Republic
Area:	105,792 square miles
Population:	11.6 million
Capital:	Ouagadougou
Language:	French
Currency:	CFA franc (100 centimes)

Mali is a land of plateaus and plains, hot sand, and mild **tropics.** Northern Mali, which the Sahara Desert partly covers, receives very little rain and often reaches temperatures over 110°F at midday. The central region spans the Sahel, which is populated mainly by nomadic herders. Southern Mali enjoys a tropical climate of 80°F temperatures and annual rainfall of about 35 inches—most of it falling between July and October.

Southern Malians farm the land, growing corn, millet, cassava, sorghum, rice, and yams on the fertile soil along the Senegal and Niger Rivers. But even in the south, life is extremely hard. Very few farmers can afford tractors, modern tools, or fertilizers, and most of them struggle to grow enough food for their families.

When there is enough rain, farmers in the south grow peanuts, cotton, and sugarcane for export, and fishing crews catch carp, catfish, and perch from the main rivers for export to neighboring countries. Mali has large reserves of iron ore, gold, copper, bauxite, uranium, manganese, phosphates, and salt, but only salt, phosphates, and a small amount of gold are excavated. Radical investment is needed to develop these resources. Manufacturing provides jobs for about 10 percent of Mali's people, who produce textiles, leather goods, processed foods, and cement. The country depends heavily on foreign aid, especially from France, which ruled Mali until independence in 1960.

Surrounded by Niger, Mali, and the coastal states of Côte d'Ivoire, Ghana, Togo, and Benin, Burkina Faso is one of the poorest and least-developed countries in Africa. Formerly the French colony of Upper Volta, this West African country gained independence in 1960 and later changed its name to Burkina Faso, meaning "land of the honest people."

The landscape consists mostly of wooded grasslands that rise to 2,300 feet above sea level in the west. The soil is poor and the climate is dry, especially in the north where most of the people herd livestock. Cattle, sheep, and goats account for almost half of Burkina Faso's export earnings, and much of the livestock goes to its southern neighbors. River valleys in the south provide the best cropland. Farmers grow millet, corn, sorghum, rice, and beans for their families and cotton, peanuts, and **shea nuts** for export—primarily to France.

Burkina Faso's people belong to many ethnic groups, embrace a wide variety of languages, beliefs, and customs, and live in very distinct homes and villages. Most of the rural people live in extended family groups or clan communities, but as in other poor countries, people are moving away from the country and into the towns in search of jobs. Many young men have found work in factories or on coffee bean and cacao bean plantations in Côte d'Ivoire and Ghana. Poverty and a lack of social services have led to a short **life expectancy,** a high **infant mortality** rate, frequent epidemics, and illiteracy. Less than 30 percent of the children attend primary school, and less than 1 in 10 of the people can read and write.

Right: An aerial view of a village in central Mali. The houses are typically square, with mud-brick walls and flat roofs. Circular mud-brick silos with thatched roofs contain stored grain.

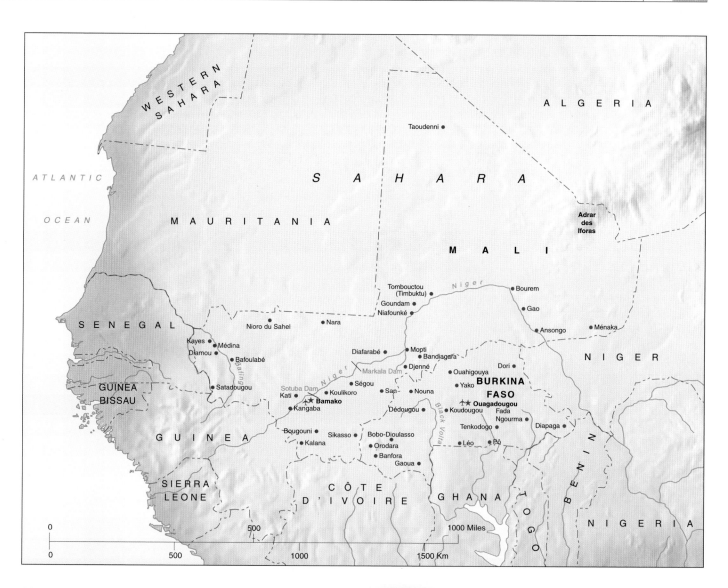

Right: Tombouctou (also spelled Timbuktu) in central Mali is a small trading settlement. But between 1200 and 1500, it was one of the most important commercial centers in Africa—a fact reflected in this old sign indicating that the town is 52 days' travel by camel from Morocco.

Niger and Chad

Niger

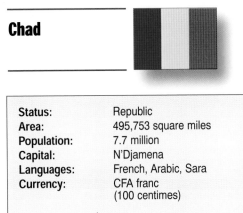

Status:	Republic
Area:	489,189 square miles
Population:	10 million
Capital:	Niamey
Languages:	French, Hausa, Djerma-Songhai, Fulani
Currency:	CFA franc (100 centimes)

The Sahara Desert covers three-quarters of Niger, one of the hottest, driest countries on earth. Sand and stony plateaus blanket most of the land, which rises to a central mountain region with peaks to 6,300 feet. The desert sees little rain, and temperatures often exceed 120°F. Small groups of nomadic Tuareg and Fulani people graze livestock in the desert during the short rainy season from July to September, moving to the thinly wooded savanna in the dry months. The savanna enjoys up to 22 inches of rain annually and is home to the Hausa, Djerma-Songhai, and Kanuri peoples, who are mostly settled farmers. Only 3 percent of the country is cultivated, but nearly 90 percent of the labor force works in agriculture. Farmers grow cassava, millet, sorghum, beans, and rice as food crops and cotton and peanuts for export. Most exported crops are grown in the southwest, on the Niger River's **floodplain.** Nigerien farmers also export livestock, meat, and animal hides. Repeated droughts in the last few decades have damaged Niger's fragile farming economy and have caused widespread suffering.

Niger's principal industry is uranium mining, but a drop in world demand during the 1980s reduced the resource's value. Nigeriens also mine phosphates, iron ore, and tin. Factory workers in cities such as Niamey, Agadez, Maradi, and Zinder process food and create textiles, leather goods, and cement. But with no railroads, few good roads, and inadequate communication between regions, industrial development is very limited. The country has large foreign debts and depends heavily on foreign aid.

Chad

Status:	Republic
Area:	495,753 square miles
Population:	7.7 million
Capital:	N'Djamena
Languages:	French, Arabic, Sara
Currency:	CFA franc (100 centimes)

Chad is a large landlocked country with few natural resources, a harsh desert climate, and little productive farmland. Ravaged by droughts and famine, it is one of the world's poorest countries. The country is torn by conflicts between the nomadic herders of the northern desert and the many different ethnic groups of the south, most of whom are farmers.

Most of Chad consists of a huge depression edged by mountains in the north, east, and south. Lake Chad, in the west, is all that remains of a huge lake that once filled most of the depression. Lake Chad varies in area from about 4,000 square miles in the dry season to nearly 10,000 square miles during the rainy months from May to October. Farmers around its shores rely on the lake's seasonal flooding to irrigate their rice and corn crops. Fishing on Lake Chad and on the Chari and Logone Rivers is an important source of food and income.

About 80 percent of the people live in the south, where up to 50 inches of annual rain enable farmers to grow millet, rice, sorghum, and cotton—the country's principal export crop. Chad's few mineral resources include oil, uranium, and natron, a sodium carbonate mineral mined near Lake Chad. But development is hampered by a lack of roads, railroads, and equipment. Chad has developed little industry and has to import most of its food and energy. France and the United States provide financial aid, and many international charities have donated food, tents, and medical aid during the worst droughts.

Right: Nomadic Tuareg on camels and on foot make their way through the dusty scrub landscape of a valley in the Air Massif in north central Niger.

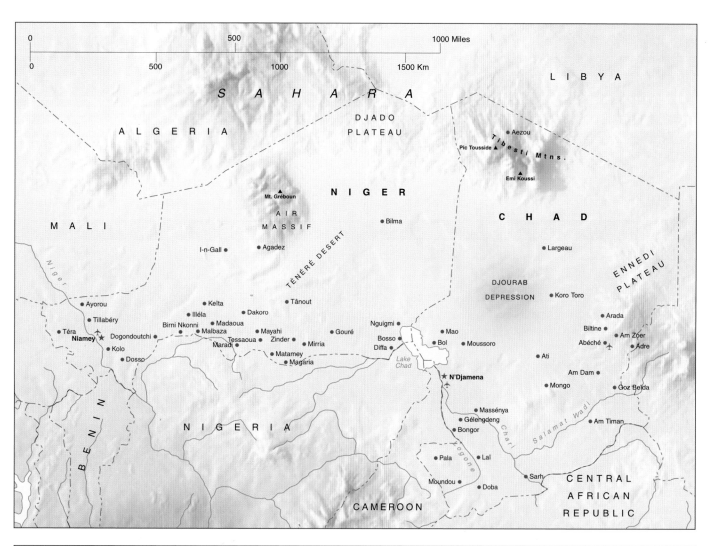

Map Labels

SAHARA

LIBYA

ALGERIA

DJADO PLATEAU

• Aezou

Pic Tousside ▲ Tibesti Mtns.

Emi Koussi ▲

Mt. Gréboun ▲

NIGER

CHAD

AIR MASSIF

• Bilma

MALI

• Largeau

I-n-Gall • • Agadez

TÉNÉRÉ DESERT

ENNEDI PLATEAU

DJOURAB DEPRESSION

• Koro Toro

• Ayorou

• Keïta

• Tânout

• Arada

• Illéla

• Dakoro

Biltine •

• Am Zóer

• Tillabéry

Birni Nkonni • • Madaoua

• Mayahi

• Gouré

Nguigmi •

• Mao

Abéché • • Adre

Téra •

Malbaza •

• Mao

Niamey ★ Dogondoutchi •

Tessaoua • Zinder

Bosso •

• Moussoro

• Ati

Maradi • • Mirria

Diffa •

Kolo •

• Matamey

Lake Chad

Am Dam •

• Dosso

• Magaria

★ N'Djamena

• Mongo

• Goz Beïda

BENIN

NIGERIA

• Massénya

• Am Timan

Chari

Salamat Wadi

• Gélengdeng

• Bongor

Logone

• Pala • Laï

CENTRAL AFRICAN REPUBLIC

Moundou • • Doba

• Sarh

CAMEROON

Senegal, Gambia, Guinea-Bissau

Senegal

Status:	Republic
Area:	75,954 square miles
Population:	9.2 million
Capital:	Dakar
Languages:	French, Wolof, Sengal-Guinean, Mandé dialects
Currency:	CFA franc (100 centimes)

Gambia

Status:	Republic
Area:	4,363 square miles
Population:	1.3 million
Capital:	Banjul
Languages:	English, Mandinka, Fula, Wolof
Currency:	Dalasi (100 butut)

Senegal, shaped like a lion's head and looking as if it is devouring Gambia, includes the westernmost point on mainland Africa. Low plains dominated by wooded savanna cover most of the land. Rainfall and vegetation vary from north to south. Annual rainfall is about 15 inches in the sparsely wooded grasslands of the north. Southern Senegal is more densely forested and receives as much as 50 inches of rain each year. Northern portions of the country have suffered from erosion, so Senegal's government has enlisted international aid for tree-planting projects to protect these semi-arid areas.

Nearly all of Senegal's people are black Africans, and about 85 percent are Muslims. The largest ethnic groups are the Wolof, Fulani, Serer, Toucouleur, Diola, and Mandingo. Each group has its own language, cultural traditions, and housing and clothing styles. Farmers in the more fertile south grow sorghum, millet, and beans for local use. Nuts are exported whole or to be processed into oil. Farmers along the country's main rivers are able to irrigate their land to produce cotton.

Senegal has a thriving fishing industry, and urban factory workers produce textiles, food products such as peanut oil and processed fish, chemicals, and consumer goods. Golden beaches attract a growing number of tourists each year, but economic benefits are not shared by most of the population. Senegal's people remain poor. Only 10 percent can read and write. There are very few doctors, and epidemics occur frequently.

Buried in Senegal like an earthworm, Gambia is barely 180 miles long east to west and is only 30 miles at its widest, north to south. The capital, Banjul, at the mouth of the Gambia River, is a busy port and the country's only large town. Mangroves and swamps line the coast and the riverbanks. Sparse forest and savanna dot the rest of the landscape.

Gambia is a poor country, with very little fertile land and no mineral resources. Farmers grow tropical fruits in the west and sorghum and rice on the higher ground north and south of the river. Peanuts are Gambia's main cash crop and principal export. The country also derives some income by transporting goods overland from Banjul to Senegal, Mali, and Guinea.

Above: Beautiful beaches of silver sand, backed by palm groves full of colorful birds, are beginning to attract large numbers of international tourists to Gambia—providing this poor country with an important new source of income.

Guinea-Bissau

Status:	Independent State
Area:	13,946 square miles
Population:	1.2 million
Capital:	Bissau
Languages:	Portuguese, Crioulo
Currency:	Guinea-Bissau peso (100 centavos)

Guinea-Bissau is a small, very poor West African country that gained independence from Portugal in 1974 after an 11-year war. In addition to its mainland territory, Guinea-Bissau includes the Bijagós Islands clustered off its coast. The country's capital, Bissau, is the principal port and largest city. Many long inlets along the country's coast allow boats to reach towns and villages miles inland.

Guinea-Bissau is mostly flat. Swamps and mangroves line the coast and inlets, providing fertile soil on which farmers grow rice. Farther inland the land rises to a plateau a few hundred feet above sea level. Farmers grow peanuts and cashews for export. Corn, yams, and beans are cultivated for local markets. Many inland farmers also raise cattle and poultry. Fish is the country's only other export, but nuts and fish cannot support the economy. More than 60 percent of Guinea-Bissau's income is from foreign aid. To restart the economy, Guinea-Bissau's government is encouraging investment in roads and machinery.

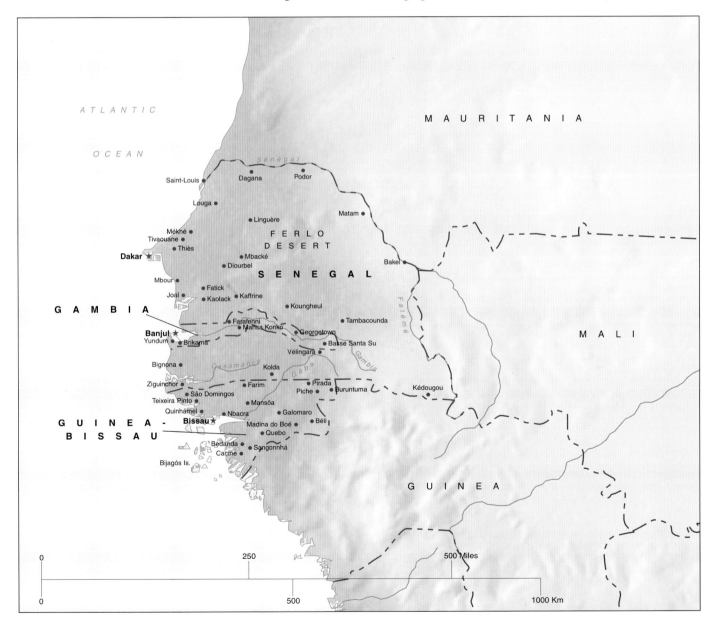

Guinea, Sierra Leone, Liberia

Guinea

Status:	Republic
Area:	94,927 square miles
Population:	7.5 million
Capital:	Conakry
Languages:	French, Fula, Malinké, Susa
Currency:	Guinea franc (100 centimes)

Sierra Leone

Status:	Republic
Area:	27,699 square miles
Population:	5.3 million
Capital:	Freetown
Languages:	English, French, Mende, Temne, Krio
Currency:	Leone (100 cents)

Guinea looks like a boomerang, extending inland from its short West African coastline in a wide arc that supports many landscapes. The coastal strip is marshy, backed by a narrow plain that rises to a central plateau called the Fouta Djalon. Upper Guinea, an area of grassy savanna, stretches across the country's northern edge. The forested hills of the Guinea Highlands dominate the southeast.

Despite its many resources, Guinea is a poor country that has suffered from inadequate government since gaining independence from France in 1958. It has a rich cultural tradition, but education and health services suffer from lack of funding, and economic improvements have been slow.

Lowland crops include rice, cassava, and bananas. Farmers in the savanna grow coffee beans, cacao beans, corn, and millet and raise cattle. Guinea's commercial growers produce bananas, coffee beans, cacao beans, palm oil, and peanuts. Guinea has about one-third of the world's bauxite reserves and pulls enough ore from the earth to comprise nearly 95 percent of the country's export earnings. But bauxite mining is hampered by inadequate roads, railroads, and equipment.

The country takes its name from Sierra Lyoa, or the Lion Mountains, the name that fifteenth-century Portuguese seafarers gave to the country's mountainous headland. The outcropping shelters the capital city of Freetown and forms the world's third-largest natural harbor. British **abolitionist** Granville Sharp founded Freetown in 1787 to provide a home for freed slaves.

Sierra Leone's coast is a 25-mile-wide bed of swamps that rise gently to a grassy savanna with scattered trees. Hills and plateaus cover the country's eastern region. The temperature averages 80°F, and rainfall varies from 150 inches at the coast to 80 inches in the highlands. Even with abundant rain, the gravelly, sandy soil is not very fertile, but farmers manage to grow rice, cassava, sorghum, and millet for their own tables and coffee beans, cacao beans, peanuts, and ginger for export. Forest hardwoods and Atlantic fish round out the country's vital resources. Mineral exports dominate the economy, accounting for 80 percent of the country's income. Sierra Leone is one of the world's leading diamond producers and exports bauxite and rutile—an important source of titanium. Recent civil conflict has hampered sustained economic activity in the country.

Liberia

Status:	Republic
Area:	43,000 square miles
Population:	2.9 million
Capital:	Monrovia
Languages:	English, local languages
Currency:	Liberian dollar (100 cents)

Liberia, from the Latin for "free land," was founded in 1816 by the American Colonization Society as a settlement for freed U.S. slaves whom the society had returned to Africa. Gaining independence in 1847, Liberia is the only country in black Africa that has never been under colonial rule. Slave descendants comprise just 5 percent of the population. The other 95 percent consists of many local African ethnic groups—the Kpelle, Bassa, and a dozen smaller groups—each with its own language, culture, and traditional territory.

Swamps and mangroves fringe the coast. Inland are grassy plains and the highlands that border Guinea and Côte d'Ivoire. Liberia's climate is hot and humid, with marked wet and dry seasons. About 75 percent of the people work in agriculture, growing cassava, rice, sugarcane, and fruit and raising sheep, goats, pigs, and poultry. Most of the produce is used rurally, so Liberia must import food to feed its city dwellers. Large estates, mostly foreign-owned, cultivate the export crops— coffee beans, cacao beans, and rubber. Liberia's miners dig large quantities of iron ore for export. Shipping, insurance, and other financial services help support the economy. Education and health services are better than in most West African countries, but there are shortages of teachers and doctors, especially in rural areas.

Right: Rubber trees in Liberia. Plantation workers cut a V-shaped groove into the bark, and the milky latex from which rubber is made oozes into a cup fixed below the cut. The trees are "tapped" in rotation, and each new cut is made just below the previous one, leaving a herringbone pattern.

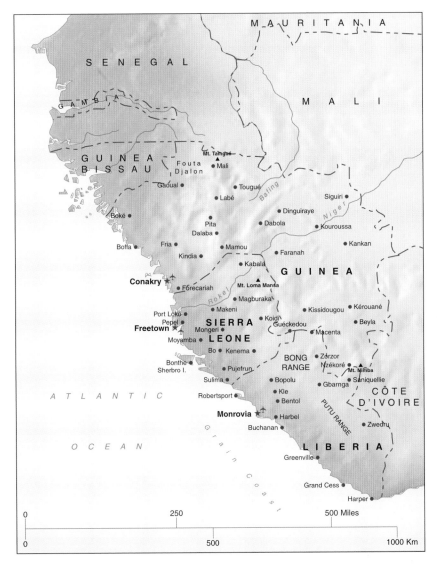

Côte d'Ivoire, Ghana, Togo

Côte d'Ivoire

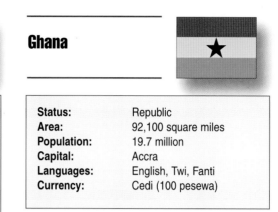

Status:	Republic
Area:	124,502 square miles
Population:	15.8 million
Capital:	Yamoussoukro
Language:	French
Currency:	CFA franc (100 centimes)

Ghana

Status:	Republic
Area:	92,100 square miles
Population:	19.7 million
Capital:	Accra
Languages:	English, Twi, Fanti
Currency:	Cedi (100 pesewa)

Côte d'Ivoire—the Ivory Coast—was named by fifteenth-century French seafarers who traded for ivory in the plentiful jungles of West Africa. The territory was a French colony from 1893 until it gained independence in 1960. Côte d'Ivoire has been the country's official name since 1986.

The land has four distinct regions—a coastal strip of sandbars and lagoons, a belt of tropical rain forest 95 to 185 miles wide, a broad wooded savanna in the north, and highlands in the west. The country's climate ranges from hot, wet, and humid near the coast to mild, dry, and variable in the hills.

More than 60 ethnic groups, practicing an abundance of languages and cultures, inhabit Côte d'Ivoire. Most of the people are farmers who live in small villages and produce cassava, corn, rice, and yams for home use and coffee beans, cacao beans, sugarcane, palm oil, cotton, pineapples, and rubber for export. Industries include oil refining, textiles, timber, fishing, and processing of sugar, palm oil, and fish products. After 1960 Côte d'Ivoire built on the French legacy of roads, railways, industrialization, and strong educational and health services, becoming one of West Africa's strongest economies. Even so, falling world prices and reduced financial aid from France have caused economic difficulties. Although the official capital since 1983, Yamoussoukro shares some governmental functions with the former capital of Abidjan.

Fifteenth-century Portuguese explorers found this West African country so rich in gold that they dubbed it the Gold Coast. After periods as a Portuguese, a Dutch, and a British colony, Ghana became in 1957 the first black African colony to achieve independence.

Ghana's altitude changes very little from its coast to its northern border with Burkina Faso. Dense rain forests cover the southwestern region and provide valuable tropical hardwoods such as mahogany for export. Grassy savanna covers much of rest of the country. Confined by the Akosombo Dam, Lake Volta in east central Ghana is one of the largest artificial lakes in the world. The dam provides hydroelectric power for Ghana's towns and a large aluminum smelting plant at Tema. Ghana also exports electricity to Togo and Benin.

Ghana, like Côte d'Ivoire, went through a period of prosperity, but political changes and falling prices for cacao beans—the country's principal export—and other agricultural products have left the country with huge debts. Ghana must continue to develop industries such as food processing, textiles, timber and furniture making, cement, and mineral exports.

Ghana's education system is one of the best in black Africa, and state-funded health services keep life expectancy and infant mortality rates close to the average for the continent.

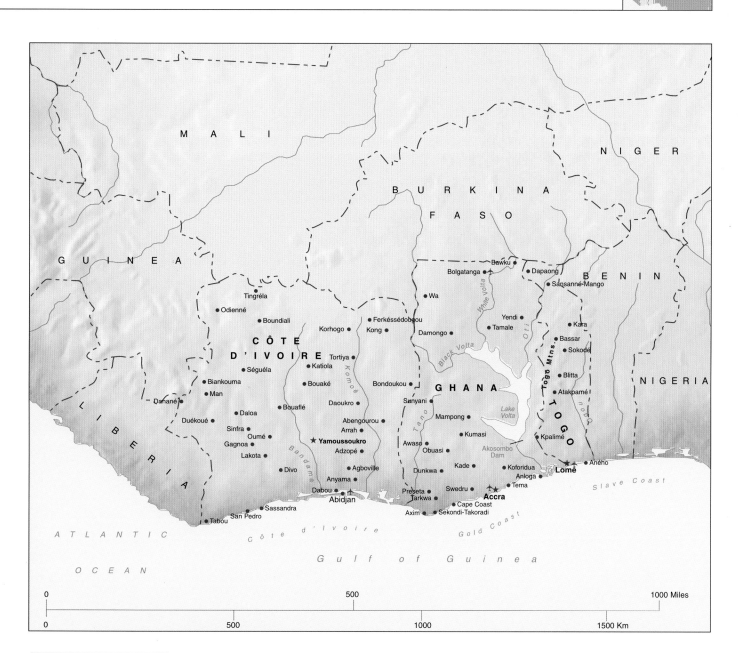

Togo

Status:	Republic
Area:	21,927 square miles
Population:	4.5 million
Capital:	Lomé
Languages:	French, Ewe
Currency:	CFA franc
	(100 centimes)

Just 365 miles north to south and less than 90 miles across at its widest, Togo is one of Africa's smallest countries. Formerly part of German Togoland and once a United Nations **trusteeship** administered by France, Togo gained independence in 1960.

The Togo Mountains dominate the country's western edge then angle across the center, dividing the country in two. South of the hills, a plateau covered in grasslands and hardwoods slopes down to a coastal plain dotted with swamps and palm forests. To the north, rolling savanna and thorny scrub extend to the Burkina Faso border.

Most of the people are small-scale farmers who grow cassava, millet, corn, rice, yams, and beans to feed their families. Larger farms produce coffee beans, cacao beans, peanuts, palm oil, and cotton for export. Livestock and fishing contribute to the food supply. Phosphates, mined in the southeast, are Togo's principal mineral export.

Benin and Nigeria

Benin

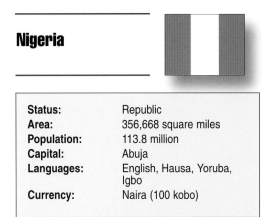

Status:	Republic
Area:	43,483 square miles
Population:	6.2 million
Capital:	Porto-Novo
Language:	French
Currency:	CFA franc (100 centimes)

Nigeria

Status:	Republic
Area:	356,668 square miles
Population:	113.8 million
Capital:	Abuja
Languages:	English, Hausa, Yoruba, Igbo
Currency:	Naira (100 kobo)

Looking somewhat like a turkey drumstick, this former French colony in West Africa gained its independence in 1960 and changed its name from Dahomey to Benin in 1975. Porto-Novo is the capital city, but Cotonou, the largest city and principal port, is the main business, cultural, and administrative center.

Sandy beaches and lagoons extend along the short coastline. No natural harbors exist, so ships must anchor offshore or alongside two long jetties built out to sea at Cotonou. Most of southern Benin is flat and forested, with areas of marshland. Savanna grasslands in the north rise to hills 2,000 feet above sea level in the northwest. The south is hot and humid throughout the year, while northern Benin enjoys a seasonal climate with a cooler, drier winter.

The Beninese are descended from a variety of ethnic backgrounds, and many follow traditional **animist** religions. About half the population works in agriculture. Farmers in the sparsely populated north herd livestock or grow cotton—the country's most significant export. Some southern farmers grow just enough to feed their families, but others produce palm kernels—the country's most valuable food export—as well as coffee beans, cacao beans, tobacco, and shea nuts. Benin produces some gold, oil, and limestone but has little industry and depends largely on foreign aid, principally from France.

Nearly 114 million people live in Nigeria, making it Africa's most populous country. Abuja, in the country's center, was chosen as the new capital in 1991, but the former capital city of Lagos—the largest city south of the Sahara—is Nigeria's commercial and industrial hub.

The Niger and Benue Rivers cut this West African country into three triangles. High grassy plains fill the upper triangle, dropping to the flat, fertile lowlands of the Sokoto River in the northwest and the dry, sandy Chad Basin in the northeast. Highlands south of the Niger and Benue rise to about 1,900 feet in the west and to more than 5,000 feet on Nigeria's eastern border. Forested lowlands extend about 100 miles inland from coastal swamps and lagoons and from the huge fan-shaped delta of the Niger. Nigeria's rainy season extends from April to October. The remainder of the year is considered the dry season. Rainfall and temperature vary considerably, from 150 inches of rain and 80°F at the coast to less than 30 inches and 105°F in the north.

Nigeria is home to more than 250 ethnic groups, the largest of which are the Hausa and Fulani in the north, the Yoruba in the southwest, and the Igbo in the southeast. About 75 percent of Nigerians live in rural areas and depend on agriculture, but Nigeria also has a large urban population living in cities such as Lagos, Ibadan, Kano, Enugu, Kaduna, Zaria (home of the country's largest university), and Port Harcourt—the country's second port after Lagos.

Petroleum is Nigeria's principal resource and the economy's mainstay. Most of the oil fields are in the southwest and in offshore waters. Tin and columbite (used in steel making) are mined in the central highlands. Miners also extract coal, gas, iron ore, lead, and zinc. Nigeria's coastal waters, lakes, and rivers produce an abundance of fish, and the lowland forests yield valuable timbers. These resources support a range of industries including oil refining, food processing, and the production of cement, chemicals, fertilizers, textiles, and steel. Most farms in Nigeria are small family businesses that raise crops and livestock for local use. Larger farms concentrate on export crops—the most important being cacao beans, palm oil, peanuts, and rubber.

Right: With her baby tied securely to her back, a Nigerian woman sweeps up corn. Her brightly colored wraparound skirt and loose turban are traditional women's dress in rural areas. Rural men wear loose robes or loose-fitting jackets with short or long trousers.

NIGER

BURKINA
FASO

Wurno
Rima
Sokoto
Katsina
Argungu
Sokoto
Kaura Namoda
Birnin Kebbi
Gusau
Mada
Nguru
Gashua
Ngurtuwa
L. Chad
Jega
Kano
Gumel
Hadejia
CHAD
Hadejia
Garko
Azare
Jajere
BASIN
Dikwa
Kandi
NIGERIA
Funtua
Potiskum
Maiduguri
Gidan Kaya
Zaria
Natitingou
Miya
Dukku
Biu
Asari
Mubi
BENIN
Kontagora
Kaduna
Bauchi
Gombe
Deba Habe
Djougou
Kainji Dam
Kaduna
Minna
Kafanchan
Jos
Kumo
Pindiga
Kishi
Lere
Numan
Yola
Parakou
Igboho
Lafiagi
Bida
Abuja
Keffi
Ilorin
Shaki
Lafia
Ila
Ogbomosho
Iseyin
Oshogbo
Kabba
Lokoja
Makurdi
Ibi
Save
Oyo
Iwo
Ede
Ado-Ekiti
Savalou
Ibadan
Ife
Ikerre
Wukari
Gboko
Abeokuta
Akure
Owo
Idah
Gashaka
Abomey
Ifon
Enugu
Abakaliki
Gotel
Mtns.
Ijebu-Ode
Mushin
Epe
Asaba
Cotonou
Lagos
Benin City
Onitsha
Porto-
Novo
Sapele
Umuahia
Ugep
CAMEROON
Warri
Omoko
Forcados
Yenagoa
Aba
Calabar
Port Harcourt
Oron

TOGO

Mékrou
Niger
Sokoto
Hadejia
Komadugu Yobe
Gongola
Mandara Mtns.
Shebshi Mtns.
Benue
Ouémé
Mono
Slave Coast
Bight of Benin
Niger Delta
Gulf of Guinea
Bight of Biafra
Bioko
(Equatorial Guinea)

| 0 | | 250 | | 500 Miles |
| 0 | 500 | | 1000 Km | |

Cameroon and the Central African Republic

Cameroon

Status:	Republic
Area:	183,568 square miles
Population:	15.5 million
Capital:	Yaoundé
Languages:	English, French
Currency:	CFA franc (100 centimes)

After World War I (1914-1918), the **League of Nations** declared the former German **protectorate** of Cameroon a trusteeship that France and Britain would govern. In 1960 French Cameroon achieved independence. A year later, the southern portion of British Cameroon voted to join the new republic, while the northern section became affiliated with Nigeria.

A range of hills and mountains runs along Cameroon's western edge, from Lake Chad in the north to Mount Cameroon, the country's highest point at 13,353 feet above sea level. A forested plateau in the country's middle drops to dry savanna in the north, tropical rain forest in the south, and a coastal plain in the southwest. Annual rainfall ranges from 400 inches in the west to 15 inches in the north.

Climate and terrain determine how people live. People on the savanna—Hausa, Fulani, and related groups, most of whom are Muslim—herd livestock and grow grain. The Bamileke inhabit the western highlands, while the Doula, Ewondo, and Fang occupy the central and southern areas. Most are settled farmers, growing cassava, corn, and yams for their families and bananas, coffee beans, cacao beans, cotton, rubber, and peanuts for export. Petroleum for oil processing and bauxite for making aluminum are important mineral exports and drive two of Cameroon's major industries. Good transportation systems, hydropower from the Sanaga River, a deepwater port at Douala, and a broad range of manufacturing industries contribute to the country's economic health. As one of the more developed African nations, Cameroon offers its people advanced health and educational services.

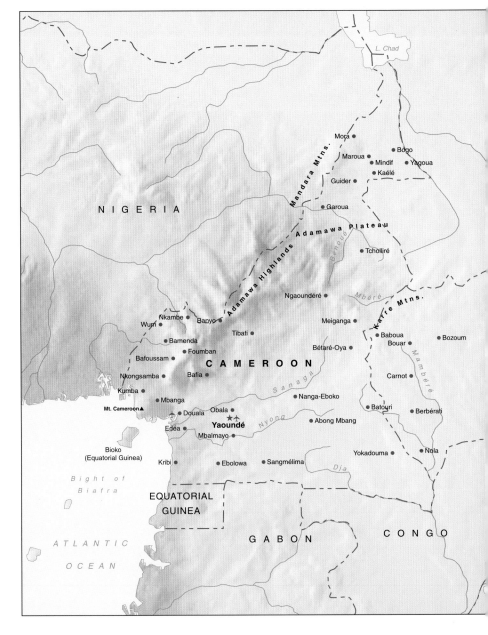

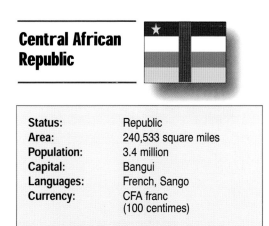

Left: Beehive-shaped granaries in a village in the Mandara Mountains of northern Cameroon are used to store millet. The intricately woven caps of the granaries can be lifted off to pour in the grain.

Right: Hardwoods are one of the Central African Republic's few natural resources.

Central African Republic

Status:	Republic
Area:	240,533 square miles
Population:	3.4 million
Capital:	Bangui
Languages:	French, Sango
Currency:	CFA franc (100 centimes)

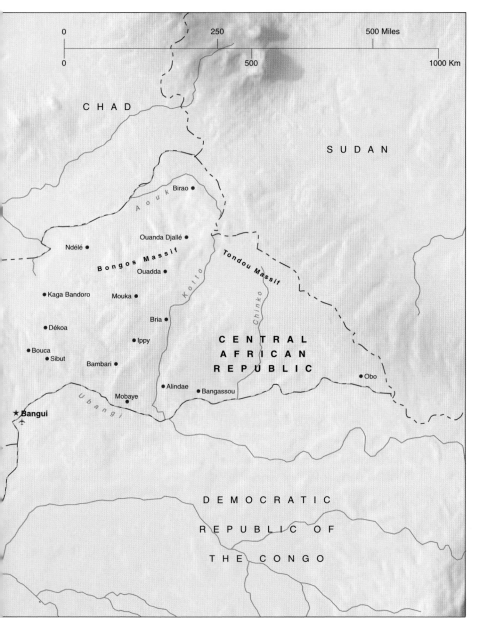

This landlocked country in Africa's middle was formerly a French colony. It achieved independence in 1960, but the following years were turbulent. David Dacko, the country's first elected president, was forced from office in 1966 by Jean-Bedel Bokassa. Bokassa ruled for more than a decade as a self-crowned emperor but was deposed in 1979 by Dacko's supporters, who put Dacko back in charge. Several years later, Dacko was overthrown by the military. The Central African Republic has returned to democratic rule under a new constitution. But with few roads, no seaport, and very little industry, the country is one of the poorest and least developed in Africa. It still relies heavily on financial aid from France.

Tropical savanna grasslands, 2,000 to 3,000 feet above sea level, cover most of the country. Rain forests lie in the south, and dry savanna is on the country's borders with Chad and Sudan. The country's low altitude keeps the average temperature near 80°F and annual rainfall at about 54 inches.

Most Central Africans are farmers who take advantage of the mild climate to grow enough food for themselves. People only keep cattle in areas where there are no **tsetse flies**, because the flies transmit deadly diseases to cattle, horses, and humans. Coffee beans, cotton, and **sisal**—the principal cash crops— are exported by ship through Bangui, the capital and principal river port. The country also exports tropical hardwoods, diamonds, and some gold, but most of the country's mineral resources lie untouched.

Equatorial Guinea, São Tomé and Príncipe, Gabon

Equatorial Guinea

Status:	Republic
Area:	10,830 square miles
Population:	400,000
Capital:	Malabo
Languages:	Spanish, Fang
Currency:	CFA franc (100 centimes)

São Tomé and Príncipe

Status:	Independent State
Area:	371 square miles
Population:	200,000
Capital:	São Tomé
Language:	Portuguese
Currency:	Dobra (100 centavos)

Gabon

Status:	Republic
Area:	103,347 square miles
Population:	1.2 million
Capital:	Libreville
Languages:	French, Fang, Eshira
Currency:	CFA franc (100 centimes)

Equatorial Guinea consists of two sections—a small territory called Mbini (formerly Río Muni) on the West African mainland and five offshore islands. The capital and largest city, Malabo, is on the biggest island, Bioko. Portugal claimed the territory in 1472 but gave it to Spain in 1778. Equatorial Guinea gained its full independence in 1968.

On the mainland, a narrow coastal plain covered in mangroves bounds a dense tropical rain forest. The soil is poor, and the mainland population of about 320,000 survives by subsistence farming, by growing coffee beans, and by harvesting tropical hardwoods, notably okoumé.

The islands are made of volcanic rock, which provides fertile soil. Farmers on the islands grow cassava, yams, and bananas as food crops and bananas, coffee beans, and cacao beans for export. Fishing and forestry contribute to the economy.

The tiny country of São Tomé and Príncipe consists of two main islands and several smaller ones in the Gulf of Guinea, about 180 miles west of Gabon and Mbini. São Tomé accounts for nearly 85 percent of the country's land area and is home to 95 percent of the population. Most of the remaining 5 percent live on Príncipe, 80 miles to the northeast. The country gained its independence in 1975, after 500 years of Portuguese rule. About 70 percent of the people are Creoles—people of mixed black African and European ancestry. Mainland Africans, Cape Verdians, and Europeans comprise the remainder.

The capital city of São Tomé is the largest urban area, the principal port, and the country's center for trade. A hot, humid climate and rich volcanic soil provide an excellent agricultural base. Cacao beans, coffee beans, coconuts, copra, and bananas are the major export crops.

Gabon in West Africa is one of six African countries that straddle the equator. Libreville—the capital and main port—lies just north of this imaginary line. Libreville, meaning "free town," was named by French missionaries who settled freed slaves there in 1849. Gabon achieved independence in 1960, after 50 years as a French colony.

Sandy beaches, lagoons, and swamps line the 550-mile coast. Inland, dense tropical rain forests blanket the land, rising to rolling plateaus and hills. Gabon's principal river—the Ogooué—and its tributaries cut deep valleys through the highlands. The climate is hot and wet, with average temperatures around 80°F and about 100 inches of annual precipitation.

Gabon is one of Africa's least populated countries. People are unevenly distributed, mainly inhabiting villages along the coast and river valleys, where they grow cassava, yams, bananas, and mangoes. Many also fish the rivers and coastal waters and hunt in the forests. The land is not very fertile, so Gabon must import most of its food. The country is one of Africa's richest in terms of natural resources. Its many forests yield high-quality woods such as mahogany, ebony, and okoumé. Oil fields in the south also garner foreign income, and Gabon is a major producer of manganese, uranium, and iron. Despite a large foreign debt, the government is investing in education and health services.

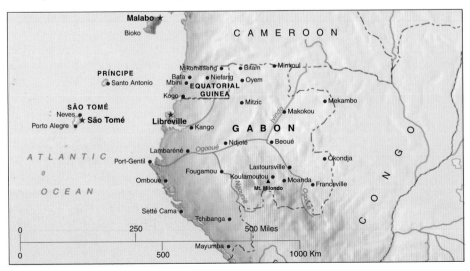

Republic of the Congo

Republic of the Congo

Status:	Republic
Area:	132,046 square miles
Population:	2.7 million
Capital:	Brazzaville
Languages:	French, Lingala, Kilkongo
Currency:	CFA franc (100 centimes)

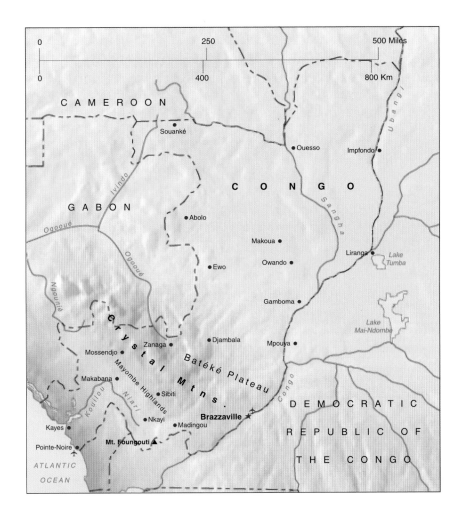

Left: The dense rain forests that cover much of Congo are a source of some of the world's finest tropical hardwood timbers. They are used worldwide for making high-quality furniture and internal fittings such as stairs and paneled walls.

For centuries the Republic of the Congo's coastline was an abundant source of slaves and ivory for European traders. In 1883 the territory became a French protectorate, and in 1910 it joined Chad, the Central African Republic, and Gabon as part of French Equatorial Africa. Congo achieved independence in 1960 and, after four decades of political turmoil, is developing into a modern multiparty state in central Africa.

The country's narrow coastal plain backs up to the 2,500-foot high Mayombe Highlands. Beyond the highlands lies the broad, fertile Niari River Valley. Grassy upland plains fill the center of the country, and dense forests and swamps cover much of the north. Congo's climate is hot and humid.

The country's principal ethnic groups include the Kongo, who are mostly farmers living in the south and west; the hunting and fishing Batekes of the highlands; the Sangha, who live in the country's northern forests; and the M'Bochi—a group once devoted to fishing. An unusually high proportion of the population are urban dwellers—nearly half the people live in Brazzaville, Pointe-Noire, and other southern and coastal towns.

Congo's farmers grow cassava, corn, rice, plantains, and other crops for personal consumption. Larger farms, mostly state owned, produce coffee beans, cacao beans, and sugarcane for export. Tropical timbers contribute to the economy, but petroleum is the principal commercial export, followed by lead, potash, and zinc. The country is more industrialized than most of its neighbors. Congolese factory workers produce textiles, chemicals, paper, wood products, palm oil, and sugar.

The Democratic Republic of the Congo and Uganda

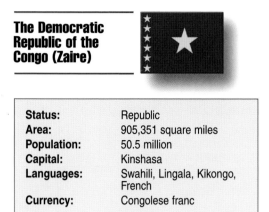

The Democratic Republic of the Congo (Zaire)

Status:	Republic
Area:	905,351 square miles
Population:	50.5 million
Capital:	Kinshasa
Languages:	Swahili, Lingala, Kikongo, French
Currency:	Congolese franc

The Democratic Republic of the Congo—formerly Zaire—is a vast country in central Africa that is joined to the coast by Cabinda, a narrow land corridor between Angola and the Republic of the Congo. Belgium ruled the country from 1885 until it gained independence in 1960. Since then ethnic violence, army mutinies, attempts by the mineral-rich Shaba region (formerly Katanga) to break away, and political and economic crises have plagued the country.

One of the world's largest tropical rain forests covers most of the northern part of the country. Conditions are hot and humid year-round, averaging 90°F and more than 80 inches of annual rain. Warm, dry savanna stretches across the country north and south of the rain forest. High plateaus and mountains dominate the east and southeast, rising to 16,763 feet atop Margherita Peak in the Ruwenzori Mountains. The 2,900-mile Congo River and its tributaries—together forming more than 7,000 navigable miles—provide the principal transportation routes for most of the country. Railways in the south link mining areas to the river ports and to the seaport at Matadi.

The country's people speak more than 200 languages. About 80 percent of the people belong to one of the main Bantu-language groups—the Luba and Kongo in the south and the Mongo who dwell in the rain forests. The north is sparsely populated. Most of the people live in the southern savanna, the eastern highlands, and the lower Congo River Valley. Each year thousands of rural Congolese move into the cities of Kinshasa, Kananga,

Mbuji-Mayi, Lubumbashi, Kisangani and Bukavu. This migration not only increases urban overcrowding but also stretches already lean resources.

The country's poverty springs from political chaos, not from a lack of resources. It produces half the world's cobalt, ranks sixth in copper production, and is the leading producer of industrial diamonds. Congolese miners excavate tin, zinc, manganese, gold, and silver. Offshore oil fields and hydroelectric power plants provide ample energy resources, and the forests yield high-value timbers, palm oil, and rubber. Farming is done mostly on a small scale for local consumption, but larger farms grow cacao beans, coffee beans, cotton, and tea for export.

Uganda

Status:	Republic
Area:	93,066 square miles
Population:	22.8 million
Capital:	Kampala
Languages:	English, Swahili
Currency:	Ugandan shilling

Europeans arriving in this small, landlocked country in the 1850s found one of the richest kingdoms in Africa. Made a protectorate of Britain in 1894, Uganda gained its independence in 1962. Until 1986 civil unrest and military uprisings caused great hardship and economic strife, the worst of which occurred under Idi Amin Dada from 1971 to 1979. In the early 1990s, a stable government supported by the people enabled Uganda to start rebuilding its economy and to attract foreign investment.

Most of Uganda is a high plateau that lies 3,000 feet above sea level, with thick forests in the south and savanna in the drier north. The extreme northeast is semi-desert. The Virunga and Ruwenzori ranges in the southwest provide spectacular scenery, with Mount Stanley's snowcapped peak rising to 16,763 feet. Lakes Victoria, Albert, Kyoga, and many others cover nearly one-fifth of the country.

The decades of conflict have severely damaged Uganda's health and educational services—a problem intensified by rapid population growth and the highest incidence of AIDS in Africa. Agriculture dominates the economy. Farmers grow cassava, corn, beans, yams, and bananas as food crops. Larger farms and plantations grow coffee beans (the principal cash crop), tea, cotton, and sugarcane for export. Mines near Kasese in the southwest produce copper, Uganda's main mineral resource. The ore is sent by rail to Jinja for **smelting** and on through Kenya to the port of Mombasa. The Owen Falls Dam at Jinja provides hydropower for the town's manufacturing industries.

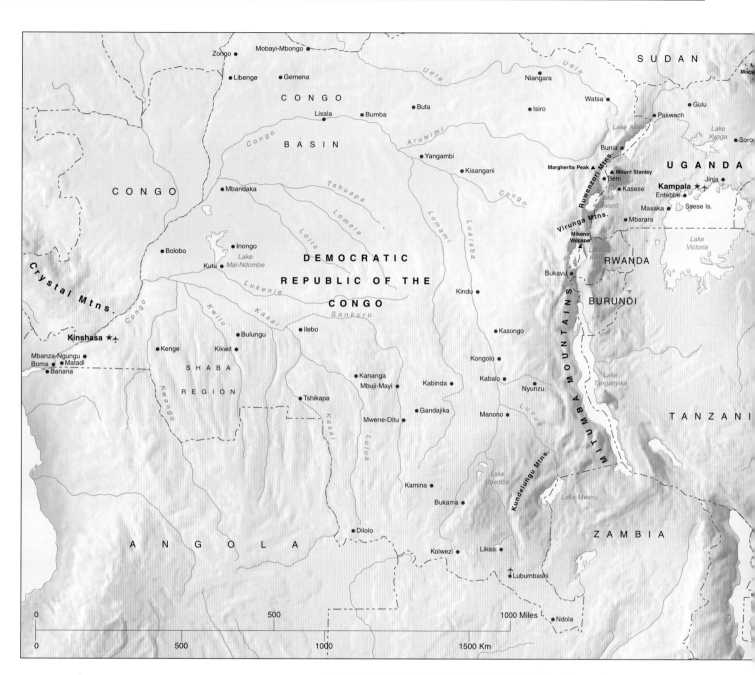

Right: The forests of central Africa are home to the largest and rarest of all primates—the gorilla. Lowland gorillas are found in several of the dense rain forests, but the rarest species of all—the mountain gorilla—is found only in the mountain forests where the borders of the Democratic Republic of the Congo meet those of Uganda, Rwanda, and Burundi.

Kenya

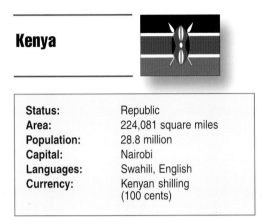

Status:	Republic
Area:	224,081 square miles
Population:	28.8 million
Capital:	Nairobi
Languages:	Swahili, English
Currency:	Kenyan shilling (100 cents)

The former colony of Kenya gained independence in 1963 after 20 years of violent opposition to British rule. Since independence, internal conflicts have continued to damage the country's economy. In 1992 the government allowed multiparty elections for the first time in 25 years. Population growth and droughts have also increased Kenya's problems.

From a narrow coastal plain, Kenya's landscape rises quickly to the 4,000-foot plateau that covers much of the country. In the west, the land rises even higher, to the 13,000-foot Kenya Highlands, which the Great Rift Valley splits in two. Mount Kenya, 17,058 feet high, dominates the south central highlands. Along Kenya's borders with Ethiopia and Somalia is a dry semi-desert region that supports very few people—mostly wandering livestock herders. More than 85 percent of Kenyans live in the southwestern highlands, where the altitude and a cool, moist, sunny climate combine with fertile volcanic soil to provide good growing conditions for both tropical and **temperate** crops. Farmland is split just about evenly between subsistence crops, such as corn and wheat, and cash crops, such as coffee beans and tea, which account for nearly half the country's export earnings. Farms on the tropical coastal strip produce sisal, cashews, sugarcane, and cotton for export. Kenya used to grow enough food to feed all its people, but the population has grown so fast that large amounts of food must be imported.

Kenya's industrial products are processed foods, paper, textiles, chemicals, and cement. Imported oil is processed at a refinery at Mombasa, and there are several vehicle assembly plants. Energy for the cities and for industry comes from imported oil, from hydroelectric plants on the Taro River, and from Africa's first **geothermal power** station near Lake Naivasha. World-famous national parks and a magnificent coast support a thriving tourist industry.

Top: The Masai are a nomadic, livestock-herding people with a rich culture of song, dance, and storytelling.

Above center: Nairobi, Kenya's national capital, is a sprawling city of almost 850,000 people. This view shows the modern office blocks along Government Road, one of the city's principal thoroughfares.

Above: The twin peaks of Mount Kilimanjaro, just over the border in Tanzania, dominate the scenery of Kenya's southern border region.

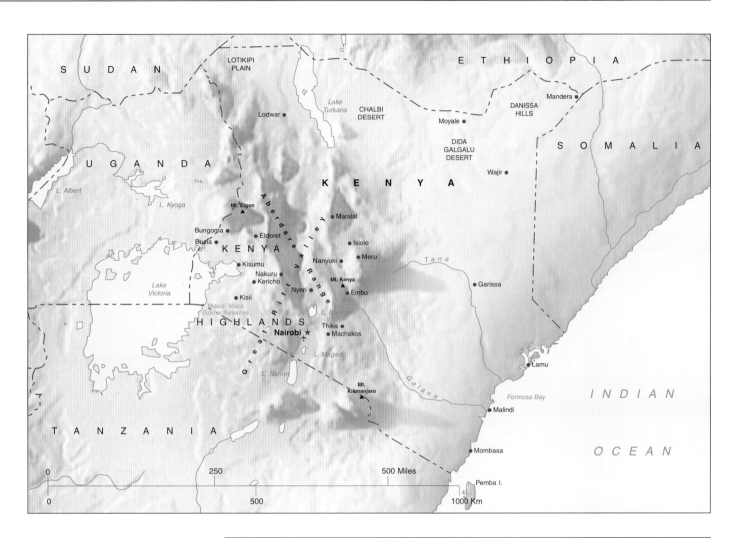

Right: Eager tourists get their first close-up view of elephants in the Masai Mara Game Reserve in southwestern Kenya. Tourism provides employment for 40,000 Kenyans and is an important source of income for the country.

Tanzania, Rwanda, Burundi

Tanzania

Status:	Republic
Area:	364,900 square miles
Population:	31.3 million
Capital:	Dar es Salaam
Languages:	Swahili, English
Currency:	Tanzanian shilling (100 cents)

Tanzania formed in 1964 when the mainland state of Tanganyika banded politically with the East African island of Zanzibar. A rolling plateau of savanna grassland, 3,500 feet above sea level, covers most of mainland Tanzania. Mangroves fringe a narrow coastal plain in the east. Northern Tanzania is hilly and home to Mount Kilimanjaro, Africa's highest peak, which rises to 19,341 feet on the border of Tanzania and Kenya. Lake Victoria dips into the country's northwestern corner, and Lake Tanganyika—the world's longest freshwater lake—forms part of the western border. Zanzibar, 23 miles offshore, is the largest **coral island** off the coast of Africa. Tanzania's climate ranges from 70°F and 24 inches of rain in the central highlands to 90°F and 58 inches annually at the coast.

Agriculture accounts for about two-thirds of Tanzania's income. Rural farmers raise cassava, corn, bananas, and vegetables, often having just enough to feed their families. Larger farms, mostly government owned, produce coffee beans, tea, cotton, cashews, and tobacco for export. Cloves are Zanzibar's most important export.

Tanzania's miners excavate small amounts of diamonds, gold, tin, iron ore, and coal, but the country is not highly industrialized. Factories produce processed food, textiles, fertilizers, paper, cement, and other goods, mostly for local markets. Spectacular wildlife, beautiful scenery, and unspoiled beaches attract growing numbers of tourists.

Rwanda

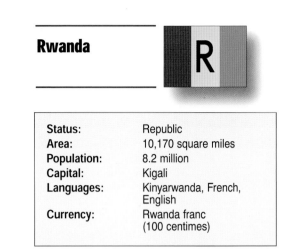

Status:	Republic
Area:	10,170 square miles
Population:	8.2 million
Capital:	Kigali
Languages:	Kinyarwanda, French, English
Currency:	Rwanda franc (100 centimes)

Rwanda's history and politics are closely linked with those of its central African neighbor, Burundi. After World War I ended, the League of Nations placed this former German colony under Belgian control. At that time, it formed the northern half of the Ruanda-Urundi territory. But the country was bitterly divided by ethnic conflict between the small but dominant Tutsi people and the much larger Hutu group—subsistence farmers with no political or economic power.

In 1962 the two parts of Ruanda-Urundi separated into independent nations—Rwanda and Burundi—but the conflict continued. In the mid-1990s, 500,000 Rwandans were massacred. Hundreds of thousands of refugees fled first to Burundi, then into neighboring Tanzania and the Democratic Republic of the Congo as Burundi also collapsed into civil war.

Rwanda is small and very poor, and it is home to many more people than the land can support. But Rwandans continue to develop their country. Tin and wolframite—the principal ore of tungsten—account for one-quarter of Rwanda's exports. Coffee beans, tea, and pyrethrum, an insecticide made from chrysanthemums, comprise the rest. The valleys are fertile, even though the higher land is badly eroded, and the country has great potential to attract tourists—especially to Volcanoes National Park in the Virunga Mountains, where rare mountain gorillas can still be seen.

Left: Covering an area of 26,828 square miles, Lake Victoria is second in area only to Lake Superior in the United States and Canada.

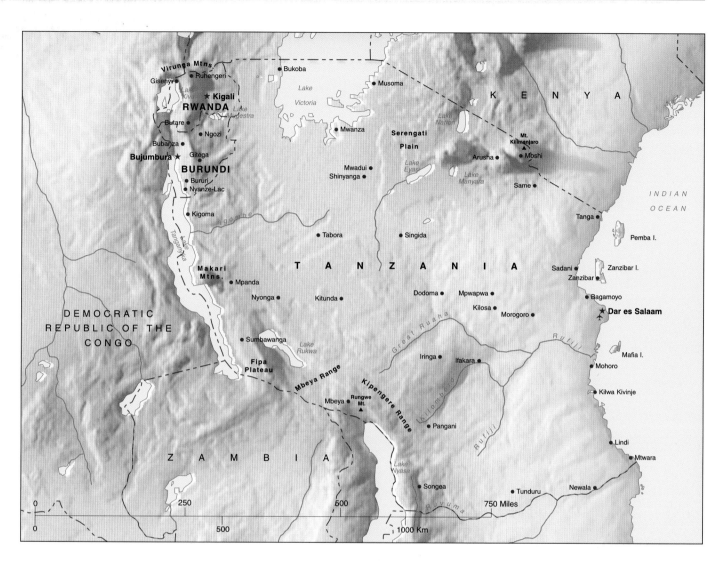

Burundi

Status:	Republic
Area:	10,745 square miles
Population:	5.7 million
Capital:	Bujumbura
Languages:	Kirundi, French, English
Currency:	Burundi franc (100 centimes)

Burundi, like its northern neighbor Rwanda, has been devastated by civil war for several decades. Hundreds of thousands of Tutsis and Hutus have been killed, wounded, or driven from their homeland in outbreaks of ethnic violence.

Most of Burundi's people are poor subsistence farmers who grow cassava, corn, beans, and yams and raise cattle for milk and meat. Farmers on more fertile land grow coffee beans, tea, and cotton for export. Robusta coffee beans, used to make instant coffee, are grown on land up to 4,500 feet above sea level. The more valuable arabica coffee beans, sold as whole beans or ground coffee, are grown at higher elevations. Fishing on Lake Tanganyika provides an important source of food for local markets.

Burundi's mines produce small quantities of tungsten, gold, and cassiterite—the chief source of metallic tin—but the country has developed very little manufacturing.

Angola and Namibia

Angola

Status:	Independent State
Area:	481,351 square miles
Population:	12.5 million
Capital:	Luanda
Language:	Portuguese
Currency:	Kwanza (100 lwei)

Namibia

Status:	Independent State
Area:	318,259 square miles
Population:	1.6 million
Capital:	Windhoek
Languages:	English, Afrikaans, German
Currency:	Namibian dollar (100 cents)

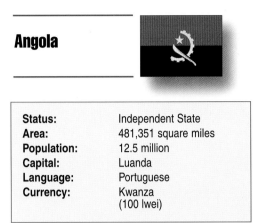

Angola is a large, sparsely populated country on the western coast of southern Africa. Its territory includes the tiny province of Cabinda in the northwest, which is separated from the rest of the country by the Congo River and the Republic of the Congo's narrow land corridor to the coast.

Portuguese slave traders established colonies on Angola's coast in the sixteenth century, and later colonists cultivated sugarcane and tobacco for the European market. Angola won its independence from Portugal in 1975 after a long and bloody war, but the principal rebel armies continued fighting until the early 1990s.

Grass-covered plateaus, 4,000 to 6,000 feet above sea level, cover most of the country, with a range of hills in the west dropping sharply to a narrow coastal plain. In the hotter, wetter north, thick forests merge with those of the Democratic Republic of the Congo. In the south, the savanna gives way to stony desert and scrub.

Decades of war have left Angola's railroads and mines in ruins and the country poor and heavily in debt. But a stable government has many resources with which to jumpstart the economy. Most of Angola has ample water and fertile soil, especially in the river valleys. The coastal waters teem with fish. The mining regions hold huge reserves of iron ore and some of the world's richest diamond deposits, and Cabinda is rich in oil. Most of Angola's farmers grow cassava, corn, bananas, and sugarcane as food crops, but a rejuvenated economy could restore the country's once-strong exports of coffee beans, cotton, sugarcane, corn, and fruits.

Above: Windhoek, the capital of Namibia, has a population of just over 104,000. The styles of its older buildings reflect the country's history of German and later South African control.

Below: Seafarers had good cause to name this the Skeleton Coast. There was little hope of survival for anyone shipwrecked here.

Namibia, formerly called South-West Africa, won independence in 1990 after 75 controversial years under South African control. Before South Africa controlled it, Germany had ruled the territory as a protectorate for 31 years.

With only five people per square mile, Namibia is one of the most sparsely populated countries in Africa. Dry rolling grasslands, 3,000 to 6,000 feet above sea level, blanket most of the country's interior. The Namib Desert—home to the world's largest sand dunes, some of which stand more than 1,200 feet high—covers the 80-mile-wide coastal strip, while the Kalahari Desert dominates the country's southeast. The narrow Caprivi Strip in the extreme northeast, ceded to Germany by Britain in 1893, provides Namibia with a land corridor to the Zambezi River.

Namibia is not fertile, but farmers in the central uplands and northern areas are able to grow corn, millet, and vegetables, and there is sufficient grass for grazing cattle and sheep. Coastal fisheries provide employment and an important source of food, but excessive fishing has caused catches to diminish. Mining dominates Namibia's economy, with gem-quality diamonds, copper, zinc, lead, silver, gold, and the world's most productive uranium mine providing much of the country's export income. Tourism is a growing industry with great potential for future development. Etosha Game Park in the northwest contains all the principal big game species and attracts many visitors each year.

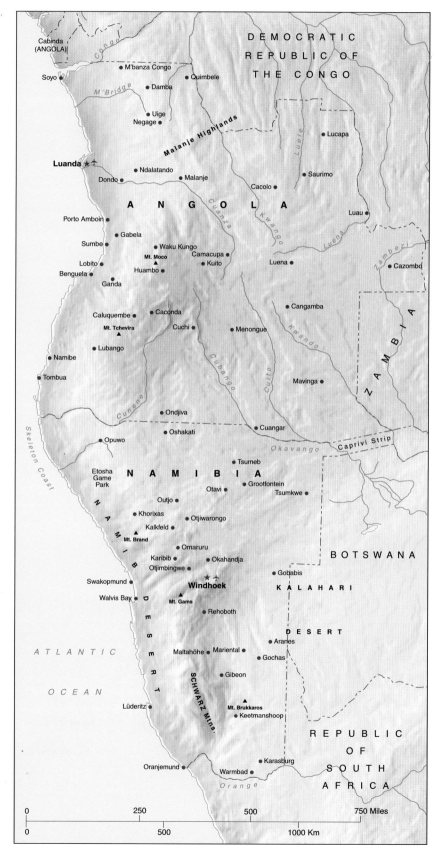

Zambia and Malawi

Zambia

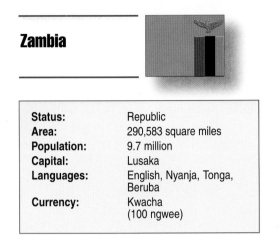

Status:	Republic
Area:	290,583 square miles
Population:	9.7 million
Capital:	Lusaka
Languages:	English, Nyanja, Tonga, Beruba
Currency:	Kwacha (100 ngwee)

Zambia in south central Africa became an independent nation in 1964. From 1924 to 1953, it was the British colony of Northern Rhodesia, and from 1953 until 1963 it formed part of the Federation of Rhodesia and Nyasaland, along with Southern Rhodesia (Zimbabwe) and Nyasaland (Malawi).

A vast undulating plateau that lies 4,000 feet above sea level covers most of Zambia. The southern part is drained by the Zambezi River and its principal tributaries, the Kafue and the Luangwa. Lake Kariba, formed by the Kariba Dam on the Zambezi, is Africa's second-largest artificial lake. Generators in the dam supply power to both Zambia and its southern neighbor Zimbabwe. Victoria Falls, upstream of the dam, is one of the world's great tourist attractions. The Chambeshi River, which flows into the marshlands around Lake Bangweulu, and the Luapula River, which flows north from the lake and then joins the Congo, drain Zambia's northern region. Most of the plateau is savanna grassland, with forested valleys full of mopani trees. The Muchinga Mountains rise to 7,000 feet near the border with Malawi.

Zambia's economy is almost completely dependent on one commodity—copper—which accounts for nearly 90 percent of the country's income. Exports of lead, zinc, cobalt, and other minerals account for most of the rest. Zimbabwe, Mozambique, and South Africa provide rail access to seaports. Kitwe in north central Zambia is the country's mining center and, like the capital city of Lusaka, is attracting many poor rural

people in search of work. Rapid urban population growth is straining the country's inadequate educational and health systems.

Zambia's farmers grow corn, millet, sorghum, cassava, and beans as staple food crops, while some of the larger farms on fertile valley soil produce tobacco, fruit, cotton, and sugarcane commercially. Some farmers raise cattle in the south, but tsetse flies prevent livestock raising in the north.

Right: Baobab trees—one of the most distinctive and typical trees of Africa—stand like sentries on the flat savanna plains of Zambia.

Malawi

Status:	Republic
Area:	45,745 square miles
Population:	10 million
Capital:	Lilongwe
Languages:	Chichewa, English
Currency:	Kwacha (100 tambala)

About 520 miles long and 100 miles wide, Malawi sits at the southern end of Africa's Great Rift Valley on the western and southern shores of Lake Nyasa. Rich volcanic soil and lake sediment provide some of the most fertile farmland in Africa, but only one-third of the land is suitable for farming. To the west and south, the land rises steeply to about 4,000 feet. Mount Mulanje, Malawi's highest peak, reaches 9,843 feet in the south.

The climate in the valley bottom is hot and humid, averaging about 75°F. Malawi's highlands are cooler at 55° to 65°F. Annual rainfall ranges from 60 inches in the north to 33 inches in the south. A warm, wet season occurs from December to March. Malawi's cool, dry season extends from May to October.

More than half the country's people live in the south, primarily in the capital city of Lilongwe and in Blantyre—the country's principal business and industrial center. Both cities are overcrowded, having seen rapid growth in the 1980s, with the influx of more than one million refugees from Mozambique's civil war.

Despite its fertile land, Malawi remains very poor. Government policies favor large commercial farms that produce tea—the predominant cash crop—and cotton, tobacco, sugarcane, and peanuts for export. Most farmers have only a few acres of land and struggle to raise enough food for their families. Factories in Blantyre and crews that fish Lake Nyasa provide important sources of food and employment. The country's lack of roads and machinery has kept it from developing a timber industry—another possible source of income.

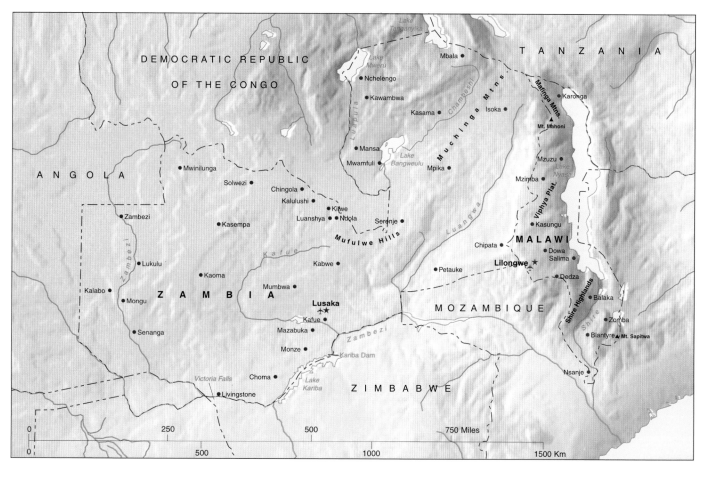

DEMOCRATIC REPUBLIC OF THE CONGO

T A N Z A N I A

Lake Tanganyika

Lake Mweru

Mbala

Nchelengo

Kawambwa

Karonga

Kasama

Isoka

Mt. Mahoni

Mafinga Mtns.

A N G O L A

Mwinilunga

Solwezi

Chingola

Kalulushi

Kitwe

Luanshya • Ndola

Zambezi

Kasempa

Serenje

Mufulwe Hills

Mansa

Lake Bangweulu

Mwamfuli

Mpika

Muchinga Mtns

Mzuzu

Mzimba

Viphya Plat.

Kasungu

Luangwa

M A L A W I

Chipata

Dowa • Salima

Lilongwe ★

Lukulu

Kaoma

Kabwe

Petauke

Dedza

Kalabo

Mumbwa

Z A M B I A

Shire Highlands

Balaka

Mongu

Lusaka ✈★

M O Z A M B I Q U E

Zomba

Senanga

Kafue

Mazabuka

Zambezi

Blantyre ▲ Mt. Sapitwa

Monze

Kariba Dam

Victoria Falls

Choma

Lake Kariba

Z I M B A B W E

Nsanje

Livingstone

Kafue

Lake Nyasa

Chambeshi

Luapula

| 0 | 250 | 500 | 750 Miles |
| 0 | 500 | 1000 | 1500 Km |

Right: Victoria Falls, named for Queen Victoria by the British explorer David Livingstone who discovered them in 1855, plunge more than 300 feet into a narrow gorge on the Zambezi River in southern Zambia. The constant roar and clouds of spray earned the falls their local name—Mosi-oa-Tunya—"the smoke that thunders."

Mozambique, Seychelles, Comoros, Réunion

Mozambique

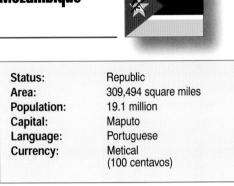

Status:	Republic
Area:	309,494 square miles
Population:	19.1 million
Capital:	Maputo
Language:	Portuguese
Currency:	Metical (100 centavos)

Seychelles

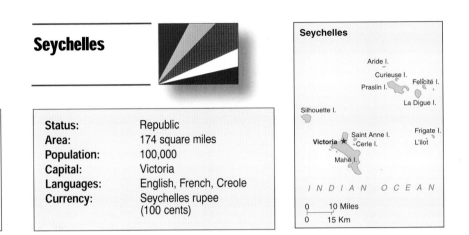

Status:	Republic
Area:	174 square miles
Population:	100,000
Capital:	Victoria
Languages:	English, French, Creole
Currency:	Seychelles rupee (100 cents)

Seychelles

Aride I.
Curieuse I.
Praslin I.   Felicité I.
La Digue I.
Silhouette I.
Saint Anne I.   Frigate I.
Victoria ★   Cerle I.   L'ilot
Mahé I.

INDIAN OCEAN

0   10 Miles
0   15 Km

Mozambique, in southeastern Africa, has fertile land, minerals, forests, and hydroelectric power. Yet life expectancy there is among the shortest in Africa, infant mortality is among the highest, malnutrition is widespread, and in many areas health and medical services are nonexistent. The causes lie in the country's recent history. Mozambique gained independence in 1975 after 400 years as a Portuguese colony and after a bloody 10-year war. A civil war that continued until the mid-1990s added to the devastation and left half the population dependent on foreign aid.

A wide coastal plain with many port cities covers half the country, rising inland to low plateaus and then to highlands and mountains on the borders. Most of the land is savanna grassland, but forests in the north contain ebony, ironwood, and other valuable timbers. Lowland plantations produce cashews, coconuts, cotton, and sugarcane for export. Inland farmers harvest cassava, corn, and vegetables for their dinner tables.

Mozambique's natural resources include gold, diamonds, uranium, iron ore, copper, bauxite, coal, and offshore gas. The economy also depends on foreign aid and on payments from neighboring countries for railroad access to the harbors at Maputo, Beira, Quelimane, and Pemba.

The Seychelles comprise about 115 islands. The larger ones are granite and are mountainous. The smaller ones are low and made of coral. Almost 90 percent of the people live on the main island, Mahé. The economy depends mainly on tourism. Small farms produce some food for local use, but most of the islands' food is imported. Tea growing and tuna fishing also contribute to the economy.

Comoros

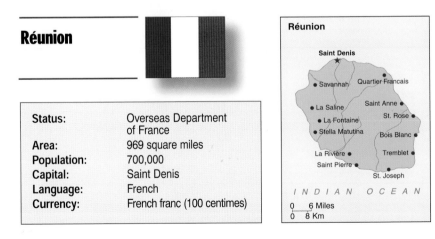

Status:	Republic
Area:	861 square miles
Population:	600,000
Capital:	Moroni
Languages:	French, Arabic
Currency:	CFA franc (100 centimes)

The Comoros Islands became independent from France in 1975, following a referendum (a vote of the people). The country is poor, with most of the people dependent on subsistence farming. Vanilla, cloves, and ylang-ylang—a perfumery essence obtained from the flowers of a native tree—are the islands' only significant exports.

Réunion

Status:	Overseas Department of France
Area:	969 square miles
Population:	700,000
Capital:	Saint Denis
Language:	French
Currency:	French franc (100 centimes)

Réunion

Saint Denis ★
Savannah   Quartier Francais
La Saline   Saint Anne
La Fontaine   St. Rose
Stella Matutina   Bois Blanc
La Rivière   Tremblet
Saint Pierre
St. Joseph

INDIAN OCEAN

0   6 Miles
0   8 Km

Réunion has been an Overseas Department of France since 1946. Before that it was a French colony for 300 years. The island's principal exports are vanilla, tobacco, tea, and perfumes.

Madagascar and Mauritius

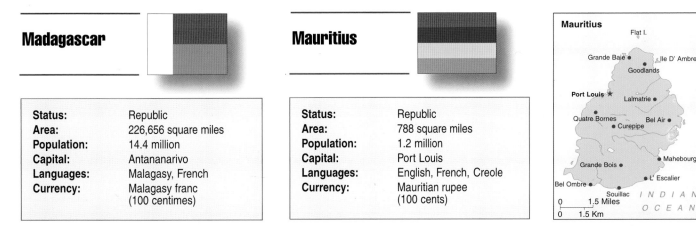

Madagascar

Status:	Republic
Area:	226,656 square miles
Population:	14.4 million
Capital:	Antananarivo
Languages:	Malagasy, French
Currency:	Malagasy franc (100 centimes)

Mauritius

Status:	Republic
Area:	788 square miles
Population:	1.2 million
Capital:	Port Louis
Languages:	English, French, Creole
Currency:	Mauritian rupee (100 cents)

Mauritius

Madagascar is actually one large island and many tiny islands separated from the southern African mainland by the Mozambique Channel. The main island lies about 250 miles off the coast and was a French colony, until it gained independence in 1960. A high rugged plateau divided by river gorges dominates the island's center. Most of the people live in this region, where temperatures average a pleasant 65°F and where 55 inches of rain fall annually. Timber cutting and **slash-and-burn** agriculture have stripped bare many of the central hills, creating extreme soil erosion. The government and international aid agencies are implementing reforestation programs to stop the destruction.

To the west the land slopes steadily to the coast—a much drier region with a smaller population that lives in the fertile river valleys. Desert scrub and patches of dry forest dominate the southwest—an area that contains some of the world's most ancient and unusual plants, half the world's chameleon species, and the unique monkeylike lemurs. In the east, the land drops steeply to a narrow coastal plain, where the main port of Toamasina is located.

The Malagasy population is comprised of many ethnic groups, mostly of mixed black African and Indonesian ancestry. The vast majority are farmers who raise cattle on the drier grassland areas and cultivate rice—the principal staple food—cassava, yams, and other crops in the fertile valleys and coastal areas. Coffee beans are Madagascar's chief export, followed by vanilla and cloves. Miners excavate chromite, graphite, gold, and semi-precious stones, but industry is under-developed and consists chiefly of processing agricultural products for export.

This remote country is in the Indian Ocean consisting of one large island and about 20 smaller ones. It gained independence from Britain in 1968 and declared itself a republic in 1992. Sugarcane plantations long ago replaced all the native vegetation. Sugarcane is still an important export crop, but the island economy has diversified to include tourism, fishing, tea growing, manufacturing of clothing, and banking.

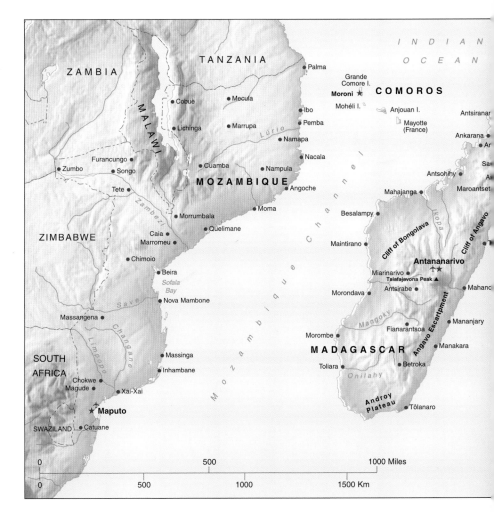

Botswana and Zimbabwe

Botswana

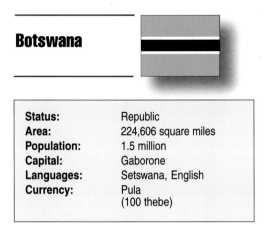

Status:	Republic
Area:	224,606 square miles
Population:	1.5 million
Capital:	Gaborone
Languages:	Setswana, English
Currency:	Pula
	(100 thebe)

This large, landlocked country in the center of southern Africa achieved independence in 1966 after 71 years as the British protectorate of Bechuanaland. It is one of Africa's most thinly populated countries, with just seven people per square mile. Dry rolling plateaus about 3,000 feet above sea level cover much of the country. Low hills rise in the east and northwest. A huge depression in the north receives the waters of the Okavango River, which flows south from the Angolan Highlands. In the rainy season, the waters spread out to form the vast Okavango Swamps that teem with wildlife. Tiny Lake Ngami is all that remains in the dry season. Streams flowing eastward from the marshes evaporate in a large salt basin called the Makgadikgadi Pans. The Kalahari Desert covers much of central and southwestern Botswana.

Most of Botswana's people live in small rural villages in the eastern half of the country, where they farm and raise cattle. Corn, sorghum, and millet are the principal food crops, but the land is not very fertile, so Botswana imports food from its neighbors. Livestock comprises the core of Botswana's agricultural economy. The country exports beef and leather, and the production of leather goods is one of the few manufacturing industries.

The discovery of minerals in the 1970s enabled Botswana to grow from one of Africa's poorest nations to one showing rapid economic improvement. Diamonds from the mines at Orapa and Jwaneng account for 80 percent of export earnings. The remainder is mostly copper from Selebi-Phikwe and coal from the east. Botswana's principal economic partner is South Africa. Botswanan exports headed to sea travel by rail through South Africa, and South African investments have long supported Botswana's mining industries. South Africa also provides jobs for thousands of Botswanans.

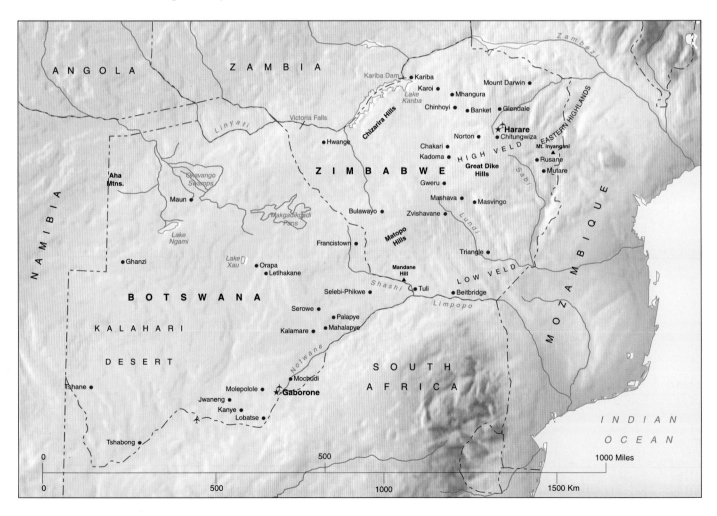

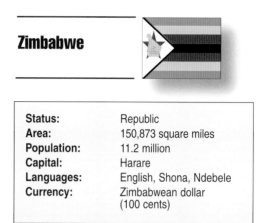

Above: Traditional Zimbabwean houses are often decorated with bold geometric patterns in contrasting colors.

Below: The Okavango Swamps in northern Botswana attract ecotourists and birdwatchers from all over the world.

Zimbabwe

Status:	Republic
Area:	150,873 square miles
Population:	11.2 million
Capital:	Harare
Languages:	English, Shona, Ndebele
Currency:	Zimbabwean dollar (100 cents)

Zimbabwe's journey to independence began in 1965, when the ruling white minority unilaterally declared independence from Britain rather than accept black majority rule. International political pressure, **trade sanctions**, and a long guerrilla war finally forced the white minority to concede. Zimbabwe gained independence under black majority rule in 1980.

Located in southern Africa, Zimbabwe has four natural regions. The High **Veld,** a 4,000-foot rolling plateau, runs southwest to northeast across the country. Large farms in this area, many of them still owned by white farmers, produce Zimbabwe's principal export crops—tobacco, cotton, sugarcane, and tea. A narrow ridge called the Great Dike stretches for 300 miles across the highlands. The dike consists of **igneous rocks** that were forced up through the surrounding rocks as molten magma. These rocks contain platinum, nickel, chromite, and other minerals, which account for about 20 percent of the country's exports. The Low Veld consists of sandy plains in the valleys of the Lundi, Sabi, and Limpopo Rivers. The Eastern Highlands rise to 8,507 feet at Mount Inyangani near the Mozambican border. Hot, wet summers and cool dry winters make some of the High Veld farms very productive, but most black Zimbabwean farmers work small plots on the less fertile Low Veld and manage to grow just enough corn and millet to feed their families.

Coal from the Hwange region and hydroelectric power from the Kariba Dam provide ample energy for Zimbabwe's well-developed industrial districts in Harare and Bulawayo. Iron and steel, automobile assembly, textiles, chemicals, and the processing of agricultural products such as leather, tobacco, soybeans, and sunflower seeds drive the country's industrial sector. Zimbabwe exports goods by rail through South Africa and Mozambique. Tourism also contributes to a balanced economy that supports efficient educational and health systems.

Lesotho and Swaziland

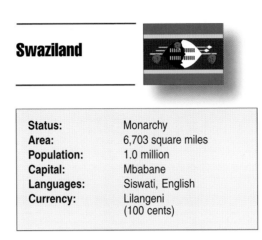

Lesotho

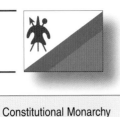

Status:	Constitutional Monarchy
Area:	11,718 square miles
Population:	2.1 million
Capital:	Maseru
Languages:	English, Sesotho
Currency:	Loti (100 lisente)

Swaziland

Status:	Monarchy
Area:	6,703 square miles
Population:	1.0 million
Capital:	Mbabane
Languages:	Siswati, English
Currency:	Lilangeni (100 cents)

This small mountainous country—until 1966 the British protectorate of Basutoland—is completely surrounded by South Africa and depends on that country for most of its food, manufactured goods, energy, and employment.

Dominating much of the country are the high plateaus and peaks of the Moloti and Drakensberg ranges that rise to 11,425 feet at the summit of Mount Ntlenyana on Lesotho's eastern border. Flat plains at about 5,500 feet encompass western Lesotho. The country's altitude affords Lesotho a mild, damp climate, with temperatures around 70°F in January—the heart of summer—and 35°F in the winter month of July. The country averages 28 inches of rain annually, the bulk of it falling between October and April.

Most of Lesotho's people live in small villages in the western plains region, with each family group of thatched dwellings built around a central kraal, or cattle enclosure. Farmers tend corn, sorghum, barley, beans, peas, and other vegetables. Cattle, sheep, and goats supply milk and meat for the table and provide wool for export. Lesotho's eastern highlanders are less settled. Men and young boys spend months in the hills riding on ponies as they move their livestock from place to place in search of grazing land.

Local factories employ Lesotho's citizens in textiles, meat canning, brewing, and furniture making, but jobs are scarce and roughly half the working-age men cross the border to work in South Africa's factories, farms, mines, and service industries. Lesotho has no mineral wealth, but its spectacular mountain scenery is attracting growing numbers of tourists.

The tiny kingdom of Swaziland is bordered on three sides by South Africa and on the fourth by Mozambique. Mountains clad in dense pine forests cover much of the country's western edge. To the east, the land drops through rolling grassy savanna to a flat, rather dry lowland plain. Several large rivers flow across the plain, providing ample water for irrigating farmland and for generating hydroelectricity.

Swaziland has abundant resources. The western highlands contain one of the world's largest asbestos mines, huge reserves of iron ore, and deposits of tin and gold. Swaziland's miners also excavate barite, kaolin, and coal. Natural forests and some of the largest plantation forests in Africa supply the raw material for wood-pulp factories and sawmills, most of them owned by Europeans. Large farms on the fertile savanna and on irrigated land in the lowland plains—also predominantly owned by Europeans—grow sugarcane, rice, cotton, tobacco, and citrus fruits for foreign markets. Meat and animal hides are also significant exports. Manufacturing—mainly processing agricultural and forest products—comprises nearly 25 percent of total productivity.

South African and European companies own many of the large commercial enterprises. Traditional Swazi farmers in rural areas grow corn, millet, beans, and other crops and raise livestock. Cattle, representing wealth and status, have a special importance in Swazi culture and are rarely killed. Rural culture and social traditions remain strong even though many Swazi people live in the urban centers and work in offices and factories.

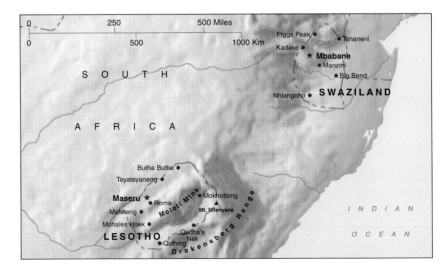

South Africa

South Africa

Status:	Republic
Area:	471,444 square miles
Population:	42.6 million
Capital:	Pretoria (administrative), Cape Town (legislative), Bloemfontein (judicial)
Languages:	English, Afrikaans, Zulu, Xhosa, Ndebele, Sesotho, Tswana
Currency:	Rand (100 cents)

South Africa is the richest, most highly developed country in Africa. It covers barely 4 percent of the continent's land area and is home to only 6 percent of its people, yet it produces 50 percent of Africa's minerals and 40 percent of its manufactured goods. It also generates about 70 percent of the continent's electricity.

The country's history has been one of conflict—from the first wars between Dutch settlers and the Xhosa people, through the Boer War (1899–1902) between Britain and the Afrikaner Orange Free State and Transvaal. In 1948 the white majority introduced **apartheid**, a policy of segregation that fueled a long struggle for black majority rule. The struggle culminated in the election of the nation's first black president, Nelson Mandela, in 1994.

South Africa's landscape is as diverse as its history. Most of the interior consists of an undulating plateau called the veld. The High Veld contains Africa's richest goldfields and much of its best farmland, where farmers cultivate corn, wheat, potatoes, and fruit.

Top right: In Swaziland, the huge reeds that grow along riverbanks and in marshes are made into thatching, baskets, and many other goods.

Center right: Cape Town is one of the world's most beautiful cities, with fine avenues, elegant shops, and parks. Its thriving waterfront serves cargo ships that arrive from all over the world.

Right: On a calm day, the Cape of Good Hope looks tranquil, but it was earlier called the Cape of Storms.

South Africa

In western South Africa lies the lower Middle Veld—cattle-ranching country. The northern Transvaal region consists of rolling grasslands where farmers grow corn, tobacco, and fruit. The Great Karroo Mountains in the south and the Drakensberg Mountains to the east separate South Africa's veld from its narrow coast. The Namib Desert borders the Atlantic coast in the extreme west, and the Kalahari Desert takes up the northwestern corner along the border with Botswana. South Africa's spectacular scenery, 16 national parks, and hundreds of game reserves attract millions of tourists each year.

Much of South Africa's prosperity comes from the country's wealth of minerals, particularly diamonds, gold, silver, platinum, iron ore, copper, manganese, and uranium. Gold earns the most export money, accounting for nearly one-third of the country's income. Oil is the only major mineral resource the country lacks, but South Africa has vast coalfields and has developed the process of creating fuel oil from coal. Coal provides 80 percent of the country's energy. The remainder is hydroelectric and nuclear power.

South Africa's exports consist primarily of minerals and agricultural products such as wool and wine. Manufacturing industries—concentrated in the Witwatersrand region and around the chief ports of Cape Town, Port Elizabeth, East London, and Durban—produce goods mainly for the domestic market. These goods include processed foods, textiles, iron and steel, paper, chemicals, automobiles, furniture, and domestic appliances. South Africa also plays a major role in the trading activities of neighboring countries. Most of the imports and exports of Lesotho, Botswana, and Swaziland and about half the goods traveling to and from Malawi, Zimbabwe, and the Democratic Republic of the Congo cross South Africa by rail and pass through South Africa's seaports.

Top left: Gold has long been one of South Africa's many valuable mineral exports.

Center left: Black rhinos in Kruger National Park are among the great sights for visiting tourists.

Left: With a total population of more than 1.7 million, Johannesburg and its surrounding suburbs and townships form the largest metropolitan area in South Africa.

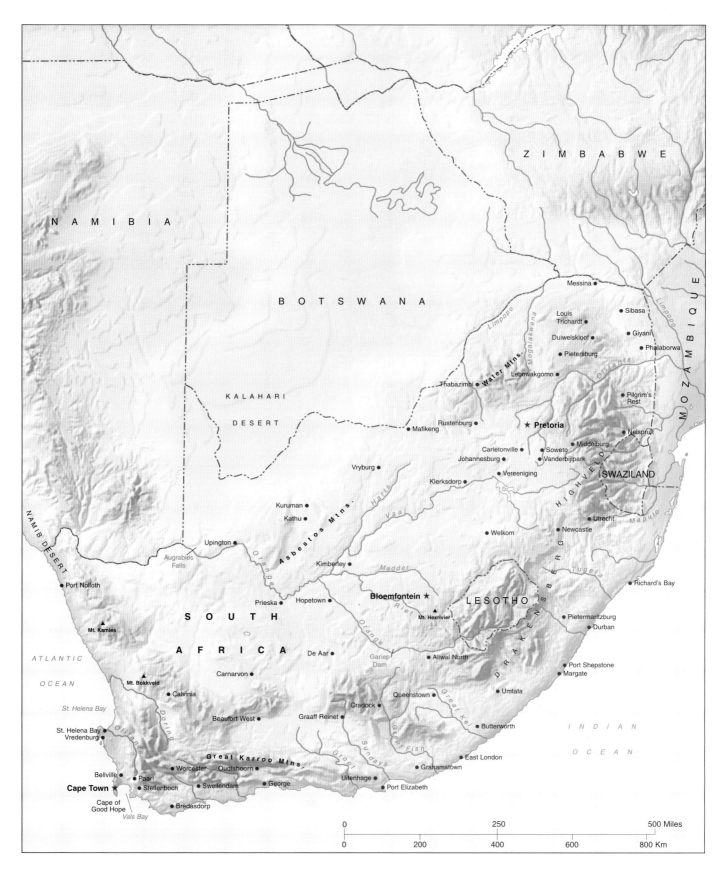

ZIMBABWE

NAMIBIA

BOTSWANA

MOZAMBIQUE

KALAHARI

DESERT

Messina

Louis
Trichardt • •Sibasa

Duiwelskloof •Giyani

•Pietersburg •Phalaborwa

Limpopo

Mogalakwena

Olifants

Thabazimbi• Water Mtns. Lebowakgomo•

Pilgrim's
Rest

Rustenburg• ★ Pretoria

Mafikeng• •Nelspruit

Carletonville• •Soweto •Middelburg

Johannesburg• •Vanderbijlpark

Vryburg• •Vereeniging SWAZILAND

Klerksdorp• HIGHVELD

Kuruman• Utrecht•

Kathu• Vaal •Newcastle

Welkom• Tugela

Upington• Asbestos Mtns. Richard's Bay•

Augrabies
Falls Orange Madder Kimberley• Pietermaritzburg•

Port Nolloth• Priska• Hopetown• Bloemfontein ★ LESOTHO •Durban

SOUTH Orange Riet Mt. Hexrivier▲ DRAKENSBERG Port Shepstone•
Margate•

Mt. Kamies▲ AFRICA De Aar• Allwal North• Gariep
Dam

ATLANTIC Carnarvon• Queenstown• Umtata•

OCEAN Mt. Bokkveld▲ Great Kei

Calvinia• Cradock• Butterworth•

St. Helena Bay Beaufort West• Graaff Reinet• Great Fish INDIAN

St. Helena Bay• Sundays East London• OCEAN
Vredenburg• Grahamstown•

Bellville• Great Karroo Mtns. Uitenhage•

Cape Town ★ Paarl• Worcester• Oudtshoorn• Port Elizabeth•
•Stellenboch Swellendam• •George

Cape of
Good Hope Bredasdorp•

Vals Bay

NAMIB DESERT

Doring

Olifants

0   250   500 Miles

0   200   400   600   800 Km

Glossary

abolitionist: a person who opposes slavery and works to end it

animist: a person who believes that there is conscious life in nature and natural objects

apartheid: meaning "apartness" in Afrikaans, a policy of racial segregation in which a minority holds political power over a majority

archipelago: a group of islands that stretches across a sea

cash crop: a crop that is produced mainly to make money and not to feed one's family

colonial rule: a time of governance by an outside power, which runs the territory as a colony

coral island: a piece of land made up of coral, rocklike formations made of billions of coral polyp skeletons

delta: a triangular piece of land at the mouth of a river

floodplain: a low, flat area next to a river or stream

geothermal power: energy produced by the heat of the earth's interior

gum arabic: a substance obtained from acacia trees that can be made into inks, adhesives, or candies

igneous rock: a type of rock from the earth's crust that has solidified from molten magma (hot, melted rock)

infant mortality: deaths occurring in the first year of life. The infant mortality rate is usually represented as the number of deaths per every 1,000 live births in a country, state, or region.

League of Nations: an international organization formed after World War I (1914–1918) to maintain peace among the nations of the world

life expectancy: the expected length of someone's life based on statistics

oasis: a fertile area of a desert that is usually fed by an underground source of water. Oases can vary in size from a small patch surrounded by date palms to a large city that raises yearly crops.

pan: a naturally occurring low place that can fill with water during the rainy season

protectorate: a territory under the authority of another

Sahel: an Arabic word meaning "coast" that refers to the belt of land bordering the southern edge of the Sahara Desert

savanna: a tropical grassland where rainfall varies from season to season

shea nut: the fatty fruit of a tropical African tree from which shea butter can be made

sisal: a strong, durable white fiber used in making rope or twine

slash-and-burn: a style of farming in which farmers clear, burn, and plow land before planting crops. The crops survive for only a few seasons, and the land is then abandoned.

smelting: the act of melting to get the pure metal of certain minerals or ores to separate away from the waste matter

subsistence agriculture: a farming plan in which a farmer produces only enough crops to feed the family, with little, if any, surplus for market

Suez Canal: an artificial waterway in northeastern Africa that connects the Red Sea with the Mediterranean Sea

teff: an African cereal grain that yields a white flour. Some teff is used to feed farm animals.

temperate: having a mild climate, with cool winters and warm summers

trade sanction: a restriction that prohibits or limits trade between countries

tropics: the hot, wet region that forms a wide belt around the earth's equator between the Tropic of Cancer and the Tropic of Capricorn

trusteeship: supervisory control by one or more countries over a non-self-governing territory

tsetse fly: an insect from tropical areas of Africa that can infect humans or animals with sleeping sickness

veld: a grassland region of southern Africa

Index